Ron,

enjoy

new

Nov 5, 2015

Saint Joseph's Seminary
Personal and Historical Perspectives

Norbert Bufka

Saint Joseph's Seminary
Personal and Historical Perspectives

The author can be contacted by
Email: norbert609@sbcglobal.net
Website: http://www.thisonly.org/

Books by Norbert Bufka:
From Bohemia to Good Harbor
Good Harbor Michigan
News from the Neighborhood
The Nicene Creed: A Reinterpretation

Pope Francis:
Pope Francis: The Beginning of a New Era
Jesus and Pope Francis: Models for Living IDecember 2015)
A Study Guide for Joy of the Gospel by Pope Francis
 "The Care of our Common Home" by Pope Francis: A Study Guide

Back Cover quote
The Rule of St. Joseph's Seminary, Part I, Sec II, #2.

Front Cover picture
St. Joseph Seminary from the seminary *Bulletin* for 1925-26.
Archives of the Diocese of Grand Rapids, Michigan.

Printed in the USA.

Acknowledgements

I owe a debt of gratitude to a number of people for helping with this book. First, Fr. Dennis Morrow, Archivist of the Diocese of Grand Rapids, retrieved many records from the archives of the seminary for me to search. Secondly, Fr. John J. Thome who lived at St. Joseph's Seminary himself for six years as a student and then as a faculty member for another nineteen years.

I thank my wife, Sue, for her help in driving to Grand Rapids, reading documents for me and typing what I wanted to use in this book. Barbara King, office professional at SS. Peter and Paul Parish in Grand Rapids made many copies of documents and pictures for me. I thank Cynthia Springer, CEO and Superintendent of the Ellington Academy of Arts and Technology, for information on the Academy. Lastly I thank my classmates and others for giving me stories and details about life at the seminary as they remembered it. I especially thank those who shared how seminary life impacted their lives after leaving the seminary.

Table of Contents

Introduction

St. Joseph's Seminary was a boarding school for boys and young men who wished to become priests of the Roman Catholic Church for the Diocese of Grand Rapids, Michigan. This minor seminary was owned and operated by the Diocese.

Prior to the Second Vatican Council (1962-1965) the traditional training in preparation for the Catholic priesthood was twelve years, including four years of high school and eight years of college. A minor seminary included the four years of high school and two years of college. A major seminary comprised two more years of college and four years of theology. Not all seminaries followed this pattern but St. Joseph's was a minor seminary and followed this model. I was a student there from 1956-1961 when I graduated.

The *Bulletin* for St. Joseph's Seminary for 1955 included this comment: "Only students who have the intention of preparing themselves for the priesthood and who give good hope of acquiring suitability for a priestly vocation were admitted and allowed to remain."

Most of the students were from the Diocese of Grand Rapids but students from the Saginaw and Lansing dioceses were encouraged to attend since those dioceses did not have a seminary. The Detroit Archdiocese had Sacred Heart Seminary, both a minor and major seminary. It still exists today for post high school students. A seminary for high school students is generally no longer part of a seminarian's training.

St. Joseph's Seminary on Burton Street was originally built for about 100 students, but that number was exceeded in the 1920's. In the 1940's the enrollment grew rapidly and surpassed 200 in 1955. This growth spurred major changes at the campus.

This book focuses on the period I lived there as a teenager in 1956-1961. Much of the information about the daily schedule, the Rule, curriculum, and other such practices in the seminary are taken mostly from a school Bulletin during the 1950's and early 1960's unless otherwise noted. I have also included the entire *Rule* of life for seminarians in Appendix A. Other original sources for information include the student newspaper which was published from 1922 to 1969, except for 1933-1938.

This book is primarily about St. Joseph's Seminary as an institution but I have woven into it my personal story and memories as well as those of others. It has been a joy for me to research and write this book as there are many wonderful memories of St. Joe's and the guys I met there. Writing this book also helped me sort out the conflicting memories that came along with it. If you were a student there, I hope reading this book does the same for you. If you weren't, perhaps it will shed some light on what life in the Catholic Church was like prior to the 1960's.

My classmate, Bob Lesinski, put together a presentation of life at St. Joe's and published it on YouTube. Enjoy!
Part 1: http://www.youtube.com/watch?v=fUgOPVfqu1c
Part 2: http://www.youtube.com/watch?v=N7REV0ZhaN4&NR=1

Main Building from Burton Street

1 Pondering the Seminary

In the winter and spring of 1954-55, priests, Catholic teachers (mostly nuns), and parents were asking their eighth grade boys, students, and sons to consider enrolling at St. Joseph's Seminary in Grand Rapids, Michigan to begin a twelve year program of studies and formation ending in ordination to the Catholic priesthood.

This asking and prodding of young boys was going on all over the United States and, indeed, at least in the western world, since the Council of Trent in the sixteenth century which established seminaries and the rules governing them.

My pastor, Fr. Thaddeus (Ted) Sniegowski, was doing exactly that in my St. Joseph's mission church in Bohemian Settlement near Maple City, Michigan. He asked me, "Would you like to go to the seminary and study to be a priest?" I liked being an altar boy and going to Mass. I learned my Latin prayers well and was reverent in church. The question did not surprise me.

Norbert at age 13

I had in fact pretended to be a priest at home by wearing my mother's long, black dress in fourth grade. Today that sounds very strange and speaks of transvestism but a priest wore a black dress then and some are returning to that practice today. It was called a cassock, however, and not a dress and with it the priest wore a Roman collar. It was very distinctive garb and was very symbolic of the Roman Catholic Church for many centuries. One only needs to find the old movie, *Going My Way*, and watch Bing Crosby in his cassock and collar.

I thought seriously about Fr. Ted's question. My family were members of St. Joseph's. The church building was erected in 1884 but it never had enough members to have its own pastor. It was therefore called a mission church and was served by priests from other parishes as far away as Frankfort, Michigan. When I was younger, the priest came from St. Philip's in Empire, where I celebrated my first communion, but in 1951 the bishop changed St. Rita's parish in Maple City, also a mission, into a parish with a resident pastor with St. Joseph's as its mission church. Fr. Ted was the first pastor. The priest who had previously served St. Joseph was a beloved Bohemian, Fr. Joseph Bocek from Empire.

St. Joseph Church

During eighth grade I pondered the question posed by Fr. Ted and talked about it with my parents. Of course most parents then were ecstatic to have a son become a priest. Mom told me about her cousin, Fr. Conrad Louis, who had become a Benedictine priest. Although I never met him, he was in some ways an inspiration to me. I did correspond with him a few times. He eventually became the abbot at St. Meinrad Seminary in Indiana.

At the time, I was growing up on a farm in Leelanau County which my grandfather purchased in 1880. The farm is now an historic site in the Sleeping Bear Dunes national Lakeshore.

Bufka Farm 1958

I decided not to go to the seminary. I am sure one of the biggest reasons was fear. I was afraid to be 150 miles away from home without knowing a single person. I also remember a silly reason for not going to the seminary that year. Leland School, which I attended for the previous eight years, was

4

building an addition and I wanted to experience that new space. I also signed up for Agriculture 1 as my elective along with the required algebra, English, world history, and biology. Taking five classes was easy for me, especially since the agriculture class was an easy one. I also chose not to be on the basketball team, even though I had been on it in seventh and eighth grades.

I struck up a close friendship with Duane Bardenhagen, a Lutheran, and we had many interesting and enjoyable conversations about religion. I learned that Lutherans were not evil people but were very much like people in my family. Religion was very clearly important to me and I had already decided I did not want to be a farmer.

In the summer of 1955, Fr. Joseph Wiekierak became my pastor. I continued to serve Mass and he, too, asked me about going to the seminary. Finally I decided I would enter the seminary. I would overcome my fear and with help from my pastor take the plunge. This meant starting a year later than most of my classmates. I didn't realize the implications of the delay until later.

Fr. Herman Kolenda at Holy Rosary in Isadore, near Cedar, was also asking boys in his parish to enter the seminary. Dick Brzesinski, Ed Fleis, and Al Zywicki all agreed to go. Coincidentally they, too ,were entering tenth grade and starting a year later than usual.

For the school year 1956-57 St. Joseph's Seminary decided to have an entrance exam for all potential students [1] and so Fr. Kolenda took the four of us to Cadillac to take this test proctored by Fr. John Thome, a priest on the faculty at the seminary. I am happy to say that Fr. Thome and I became close in the seminary and continued that friendship later in life.

The seminary sent me the *Bulletin* for the coming year from which I learned the requirements for enrolling: I had already completed the personal application form and my pastor completed a recommendation form. Since I attended another institution, I was required to provide "a testimonial letter from" Leland Public School. Another requirement was that I be "of sound health and free from canonical impediments". The enrollment process involved submitting a doctor's report, a copy of my baptism and confirmation certificates, proof of my parents' marriage and also sent a small photograph with my name and date.

It was highly recommended that students enter the seminary after eighth grade, because "experience has shown that most of those who make their high school course before enrolling in the Seminary must attend special classes for one or more years, before they are adequately adjusted to a prescribed course of studies." [2] Because I entered in tenth grade, I was one of these students with a special course in Latin. There were no mid-year enrollments. After one semester of special Latin, I was placed in the regular second year Latin class and I also had a summer course in Latin in 1957.

St. Joseph's Seminary Main Building

After acceptance by the seminary, there was a lot more preparation. Mom and I had to buy and prepare a suitable set of clothes to wear. The *Bulletin* told us that clothing "must be plain and sober, dark in color and conservative in style. All the articles which can be laundered must be marked with the owner's name, preferably on stamped tapes. All clothing must be marked before the enrollment date. Students use laundry mailing kits to send laundry home each week." So Mom ordered the tape and began sewing one in each piece of clothing.

Students were advised to bring "adequate changes of outer clothing and underwear, one overcoat, one sweater coat, rubber-heeled shoes, rubbers or overshoes, slippers, six pairs of hose, three pajamas; bathrobe, gymnasium shoes with white soles, two white cotton trunks and two white cotton shirts for gymnasium wear; a supply of towels, handkerchiefs, napkins and toilet articles; two laundry bags, one laundry mailing kit, four bed sheets (63x99), three pillow slips, two white bedspreads, one heavyweight blanket for the size of bed, and one mattress protector. The bedspreads may be purchased at the Seminary."

I was excited about all this but couldn't help wonder what I was getting myself and my family into.

Field Day and Open House

In May 1956 Fr. Joe took me to the seminary for Field Day and Open House and I saw for the first time the place that was to be my home for the next five years.

Relay Race May 1956

An annual fun day of field and track events was a long tradition at St. Joseph's Seminary since its first full year of operation in 1921-22 at the Burton Street site. However there was a long hiatus from 1929 to 1940.[3] Field Day events included long jump; pole vault; broad jump; discus; shot put; and dashes as well as a baseball game between faculty and guest priests and students.[4] High jump and relay races were also part of Field Day when I was a student.

Field Day Games

In May 1942 the seminary decided to use Field Day as an Open House for prospective seminarians. [5] This proved to be a successful idea. In 1943 106 boys came [6] followed by "an astonishing number of 173 prospective seminarians" in 1945. [7] In 1947 there were 82 visiting priests and 120 boys. [8] In 1955 the number of priests and prospective students soared to 357. [9] In 1956 this number was 200. [10] I was one of those 200.

A Field Day Committee was on hand to greet visitors and show them through the buildings in the hope the boys would feel at home and help make them ready for entrance in the fall. [11]

On May 12, 1965 Field Day changed to Orientation Day with sports being dropped. It was a chance to introduce young men to the seminary, it was reported, [12] even though that had been happening for over twenty years.

In 1957 E. Beiter, F. La Pres, and P. Kolbiaz were key students in preparing the new equipment for the Pole Vault and high jump. "The pole vault is modeled after equipment built for Muskegon CC by Mr. H. Salisz their shop instructor.... Fr. Zaskowski was cooperative on the project providing materials, helpful suggestions, and a frequent helping hand." [13]

The program for Field Day in 1956 was:
9:00 A.M. Parade, Flag Raising Track Meet
12:30 P.M. Dinner! !
2:00 P.M. Baseball Game between Clergy and Students [14]

The students were all divided into Reds and Blues. This assignment stayed with the student for the duration of his time at the seminary. When I was a student there were three divisions because of the large enrollment. The divisons were First year, Second and Third years, Fourth through sixth years. I do not remember if I was a Red or a Blue.

Field Day scores were as follows with the winner in bold.

Year [15]	Red	Blue
1941	**122**	109
1942	103	**131**
1943	**132**	99
1944	73	**132**
1945	**134**	97
1946	98	142
1947	**134**	112
1948	107	**139**
1949	115	**118**
1950	109	**126**
1951	106	**125**
1952	**119**	112
1953	80	**150**
1954	**111**	105
1955	**147**	84
1956	**136**	121
1957 [16]	**184**	74
1958 [17]	112	**146**
1959 [18]	115	**117**
1960 [19]	**122**	109
1961 [20]	**132**	99
1962 [21]	**134**	96
1963 [22]	**212**	130
1964 [23]	99½	**132½**

Baseball game

Finally we came to the big event of the day: the annual baseball game pitting clergy against the students. The clergy could be any priest, not just faculty. Clergy fans sat on the left of the batter's box and cheered on their team while students were on the right side doing the same.

Year	Students	Clergy
1922	2	2
1923	No game rain	
1924	**10**	0
1925	**18**	5

Year		
1926	8	7
1927	5	0
1928	3	8
1929	No game rain	
1939	10	8
1940	11	1
1943	5	1
1946	12	3
1947	8	6
1948	3	4
1949	No Game rain	
1950	3	6
1951	5	8
1952	1	2
1953	9	15
1954	2	8
1955	5	5
1956	8	5
1957 [24]	2	6
1958 [25]	5	2
1959 [26]	20	0
1960 [27]	9	5
1961 [28]	16	8
1962 [29]	5	8
1963 [30]	11	6
1964 [31]	No game rain	
1965 [32]	2	1
1969 softball [33]	9	19

In the newsletter for guests at the Open House in 1957, an upper classman wrote about the need for more priests. There is a shortage of priests, he wrote, and he referred to Jesus' saying that the harvest is great, but the laborers are few. This shortage could be overcome if boys knew how wonderful it is to be a priest and what the seminary is all about. He wrote,

"The seminary is the training camp for the soldiers of God's army. We seminarians are the soldiers. It is in the seminary that we receive our "boot camp!" Moreover , we work for a Commander who promised to reward us 100 times over for all the service we do....All it takes is a generous soul." This analogy to an army was typical of the day and reflects the culture of the Roman Catholic Church at the time. This book will describe that culture in more detail from a seminary perspective.

2 Life at St. Joe's

The day after Labor Day was designated as the one for students to arrive at the seminary and get checked in. That first day for most of my class was September 3, 1955. Dave Huhn was one of those students.

Since I started in tenth grade, my

Dave Huhn moving in first day September 3, 1955

first day was on Tuesday, September 4, 1956. My family took me to the seminary which they saw for the first time. It was of course a day with mixed emotions. Here I was embarking on the course I had initiated earlier in the year. It was exciting and scary. Students, I am sure, greeted us as well as perhaps a priest or two or the Rector but I don't remember any of that. I am assuming my family came into the building with me and saw where I would be sleeping and my locker for the few clothes that I had.

My bed was located in one of the corrals on the third floor. A corral was an area of a larger room set off by temporary walls. These corrals were required by the large number of students attending the seminary in a building designed for 100, not over 200.

After I said goodbye to my family, I wandered around the place with other students so as to get a feel for the place, where things were, and how to get around from one place to another.

Our "home room" was the study hall in the west wing on the first floor where we all kept our books, papers, and other items normally found in a desk. We had regular study time and we could also go there during free time to study. We also gathered there for announcements. Such was the case in the evening of our first day when Msgr. Edmund F. Falicki, the Rector, welcomed us and talked about seminary life. "You will get up at 6:00 a.m. and you will have 20 minutes to get dressed and into the chapel. On Saturdays, Sundays, and Holy Days you get to 'sleep in' until 6:30." This remark got a little laughter from the students who were returning. We new students weren't relaxed enough yet to know the humor in that comment.

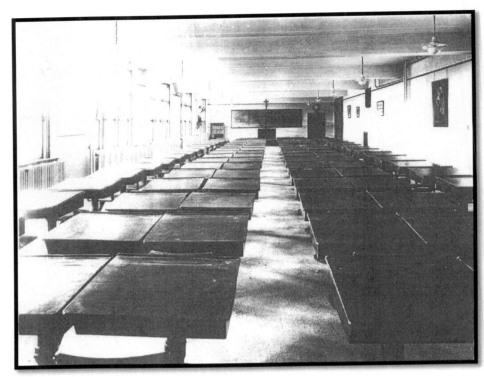

Study Hall

Msgr. Falicki also talked about being friends with everyone and not establish "particular friendships" or hang out with one person exclusively or to form cliques. While the primary message was clearly to establish camaraderie among all the students, it was also a warning against homosexual tendencies and activities.

The rector also told us we were not allowed to leave the seminary grounds for any reason without permission although permission would be granted for a visit to the museum, the cathedral, or the doctor's office. Miller's Dairy across the street was especially taboo but some students did sneak out at night, go there and return without being caught. Leaving the grounds without permission was a cause for dismissal. One student who managed this unauthorized visit to Miller's Dairy was a classmate, Jim Swiat, who later was ordained and has served the Church for nearly fifty years as a priest and pastor. In Jim's own words: "Yes - I slipped out... to go to Miller's.   Great ice cream! It was the beginning of my interest in 'liberation theology'. And now it can be told... in your book!"

Msgr. Falicki ended his welcome with a note about silence. We were expected to be silent in study hall and chapel but there was a special period of silence from night prayers until breakfast, called "grand silence." A breach of this silence could result in a "mark in conduct". On every report card we were given a conduct mark of I, II, or III. One was good, II needed to improve, and III was cause for dismissal unless corrective action was taken immediately. Guess who got a II in conduct one marking period? I was caught twice talking during 'grand silence". Everyone who knows me will not be surprised at this revelation. That was the only marking period I had other than a I rating. It was the last marking period of my first year.

In 1925-26, the *Bulletin* said, "Conduct and application are graded as Excellent, Very good, Good, Fair, Poor. A grade lower than Very good is considered unsatisfactory." In 1937-38 these ratings had changed to four classes: Good, satisfactory (advised to improve), Not satisfactory (must improve), and Poor. The grades tell us how high were the expectations. "Satisfactory" was not good enough.

Main dormitory with single beds 1925

The evening of that first day we began our seminary life with prayer in the chapel and then off to bed. After the lights went out, a classmate, John Doyle, recalled, many boys were so homesick they couldn't help but cry during that grand silence. John thought he might have been one of them. I don't recall being homesick that night but it sure hit me after I was there a few weeks and discovered how difficult the studies and the regimen were for me. After a few months I do remember not being so homesick.

On Wednesday, September 5, I began my new life at the seminary by joining all the students in a Solemn High Mass of opening. Then we began this schedule:

Daily Program

Class Days

We brushed our teeth every morning

A.M.
6:00 - Rise
6:20 - Morning Prayers, Meditation
6:50 - Holy Mass
7:30 - Study
7:55 - Breakfast
8:45 - Class
10:25 - Intermission
10: 35 - Class
P.M.
12: 15 - Visit to the Blessed Sacrament
12:20 - Dinner
1:40 - Class or Study
2: 35 - College Recreation
4:05 - High School Recreation
5:35 –Study
6:30 – Supper, Recreation
7:45 - Rosary – Benediction on appointed days
8:00 - Spiritual Reading
8:10 - Study
9:15 - Night Prayers
9:45 - Retire
No classes were held on Wednesday or Saturday afternoon.

In order to give us even more time to learn, a student read aloud from a book during the first few minutes of supper. During retreats, there was reading during the whole meal and maybe during the other two meals as well. I don't remember. One time during Lent, we were served hot dogs on a Friday and

14

all of us students were scandalized. The reading however was about "tuna dogs". Two of the books which were read are *Life and Labors of Bishop Baraga* [34] and *The Street of the Half Moon* about the life of St. Peter Claver. [35]

Sundays
A.M.
6:30 - Rise
6:50 - Morning Prayers, Meditation
7:20 - Holy Mass
8:00 - Study
8:25 - Breakfast
9:15 - Solemn Mass, Recreation
10:25 – Intermission, Recreation
11:00 - Student Organizations Meetings.
P.M.
12: 30 - Visit to the Blessed Sacrament
12:35-Dinner followed by Recreation
3:30 - Vespers, Benediction, Recreation
6:00 - Supper
7: 30 - Conference
7:45 - Spiritual Reading
7:55 - Study
9:00 - Night Prayers
9:30 - Retire

The order of the day for holidays was the same as on Sundays, sometimes with a Solemn High Mass and sometimes not, depending on the type of holiday. "Recreation" in the schedule above essentially meant free time to do whatever we wanted within the bounds of the Rule. (See Appendix A for the complete Rule we lived by.) On weekday afternoons the recreation was compulsory.

We were summoned to each of these times by a bell which rang throughout the entire building and even outside if there was a chance some of us were outside, like after recreation or leisure time after meals.

Many of us thought rising at 6:00 a.m. bordered on abusive but it was not a challenge for me. I still enjoy getting up early. In the 1920's the time to rise was half hour earlier at 5:30 with lights out at 9:00 p.m. In the 1970's it was delayed to 6:30 with lights out at 10 and even 11p.m.

Curriculum

The year was divided into two semesters with four marking periods in each one. The curriculum below reflects the time I was a student in the

1950's. Since the seminary was really a six year program I am including our courses as part of the six years rather than divide into high school and college.

Religion all six years.

English all six years.
American and English Literature were part of the English course.

Languages.

Fr. Francis Hackett teaching Latin

Latin all six years

By second year we were reading from *Viri Romae*. In third year, we were reading from Caesar's *Gallic Wars*, Books I and II. Third year included Cicero's *In Catalinam*, Fourth year: Cicero's *Pro Milone*, Ovid's *Metamorphosis*. Fifth and sixth years included readings from various Latin authors such as Virgil's *Aeneid* and some Latin Fathers of the Church.

Greek started in 2nd year and continued through sixth year.

Xenophon's *Anabasis*, Books I and II, was started in Greek II. Third year included Homeric Greek with three books chosen from Homer's *Iliad* or *Odyssey* or Sophocles' *Antigone*. I had Homer's Iliad in third year and *Antigone* in fourth year with Koine Greek (New Testament) in fifth year.

Modern Language began third year for two years.

French or Spanish was my option but German, Polish, and Italian were offered in the past. In 1959 Fr. Rose taught German as an extra course.[36] I was in that class which lasted only one semester. The Bulletin indicated modern languages were taught in the fifth and sixth years as well, but not while I was a student.

Math and Science:

Algebra in first year.

Geometry in second year.

Biology and chemistry offered in alternate years in third and fourth years.

Physics was offered in fifth or sixth year.

History

United States History in first year.

World History in second year.

While the *Bulletin* indicated courses in history in fifth and sixth years, I do not recall them when I was there.

Public Speaking all six years.

Interestingly, in 1925-26 speech class was called "elocution" in the four years of high school and public speaking in college.

Music One hour a week all six years.

Other courses

Sociology was offered at one time to fifth and sixth year students, and I remember a course in Logic, taught in Latin by Msgr. Thomas Martin. In 1922 there was an astronomy class for fifth and sixth year students. [37]

In 1939, an innovation in seminary curriculum was the addition of the senior bookkeeping class.[38]

In 1958-59 Government was added to the fourth year curriculum to comply with state requirements.[39]

Our textbooks were a long held tradition. As a result changes elicited this kind of a response in the paper in 1946:

> *"We gasped when the Genung Rhetoric text was stricken from the curriculum. We were stunned when another Latin text other than Shultz was introduced into the Seminary. But the change which recently took*

place has left us all speechless and amazed. It is nothing so common as the atomic bomb." [40]

I remember both Genung and Schultz when I was a student so perhaps this amazement caused a return to these texts.

'In 1933, under the direction of Bishop Joseph G. Pinten, alterations were made in the east wing of the seminary building and additions were made to the faculty' so that a two-year course in philosophy would follow the six-year classical program.

In 1938 the philosophy course was discontinued and the seminary returned to the six-year program of studies.

Study

As one can readily see from the daily schedule, our days were very structured. We knew where and what we were doing all hours of the day and night. This meant that study time had to be used well. As I was preparing this book and noticing our daily schedule once again, I was surprised at the few hours of study time that I really had for all those classes. My first year was the most difficult because I had to take a special Latin class in order to catch up with my classmates. The teacher decided that I and my fellow special students were sufficiently caught up by the second semester and we were placed into Latin II class. I had to take Latin in the summer as well. After that I was pretty much comfortable with Latin but that first year was especially challenging for me.

It was also challenging because I also was taking Greek I. First and most important learning was the Greek alphabet. I can still recite and write the alphabet after all these years. As a result I can no longer say "It's all Greek to me" when I come across something I don't understand!

In my second year in the seminary (third year class or Junior in high school), I took Latin III, Greek II, and Spanish I. Some of us were foolish enough to ask Fr. Rose to teach us some German also. We met twice a week for about a semester until we decided that was too much. Before we had a chance to tell Fr. Rose, he told us he didn't have time for the class either.

Examinations and grades

We had regular examinations in all subjects twice in each semester. We had oral and written tests, both surprise and announced, at various times. Educational and Psychological Tests were given during the year to enable the instructors to evaluate better the needs of the students and to enhance their scholastic progress.

In the first few years of the seminary, final exams were oral in the presence of the Bishop and clergy. [41]

Grades were based on the following schedule :

A - 94-100	Extraordinary
B - 86-93	Better than average
C - 78-85	Average
D - 70-77	Less than average
E -	Conditioned
F - Less than 70	Failure
I -	Incomplete

Students whose work was rated E or I had to remove their condition or complete their assignment during an allowed period of time, or they failed automatically. We were promoted only at the beginning of the year.

Warning and Probation

Low grades, lack of interest, or neglect of work during any semester rendered a student liable to probation. A student who did not maintain an average higher than 78 or C was warned. If a student's scholastic average was less than 78 or C, or if a student had one failing grade, he was put on probation for the succeeding semester. During the period of probation, the student was on trial to prove his fitness to carry a seminary course of studies. He was required to remove the probation to qualify for promotion in the course or for graduation.

Grade Reports

The monthly grade and conduct reports were read aloud in front of all the students.[42] While this may sound cruel and abusive by today's standards, it was probably fairly common in other private boarding schools. This practice continued until 1955-56 when most of my classmates entered St. Joe's. Neither John Mullally nor I remember them being read aloud in 1956-57, our first year there. In 1925-26 semi-annual reports were sent home to the parents.[43] In 1932 the reports were sent home monthly to the parents for their signature.[44] Later a semester report was issued to the parents and the pastor with a return certification of receipt attached.

The study habits I learned at St. Joe's helped me in my future studies at Aquinas College, Illinois State University, and Loyola University New Orleans. Those habits also have helped me in organizing my daily routines at various phases of my life and stayed with me and been helpful in preparing speeches and writing books.

Discipline

It was very clear from the outset that obedience was the primary virtue of a seminarian. Close to obedience were a spirit of "mortification, and the love of order and punctuality." [45] Obedience was also the primary virtue expected of all Catholics, so it was not unusual to find this expectation in the

19

seminary Rule. Students, too, expected obedience from others when they were assigned as prefects. The Rule says this about prefects:

> "4. *Some students are appointed prefects and are charged with certain responsibilities in disciplinary matters. They are to be respected and obeyed as representatives of authority. They shall report all infractions of discipline to the Superiors.*" [46]

Prefects for the most part were upper classmen or at least in higher grades than the students they were in charge of. Table prefects were at the head of the dining table for all meals. All the students ate together and so the table prefects were naturally sixth year students. Fifth year students were appointed if there were not enough sixth year students. Besides the disciplinary role of the table prefect, he was the one who went to the bread table to get more bread for his table. On Sunday morning there was a rush to see who could get to the bread table first as we always had frosted bread that day. The tables were rectangular so the prefects sat at one end and the first year students were at the other end with other students filling in on the other chairs available. I am sure we were assigned tables but I don't specifically recall that. I know I was a table prefect in my sixth year but I have no tales to tell about that role. Since there was a mixture of grades at each table, this assignment provided an excellent opportunity for all students to get to know each other.

Whenever we went for walks, one person was assigned as prefect for that walk.

Another regular prefect was the dorm prefect. He slept in the same area with the students in the large dorm on the fourth floor or one of the corrals in the main building. He was to supervise the minutes when we all got ready for bed and into bed. It was during a period of grand silence, so there was to be no talking ever. Any infractions were generally of a very minor nature. These prefects were fourth year students until St. Henry's was built. Since St. Henry's was built for anticipated larger enrollments, it had more rooms than were needed for just those two upper grades. Fourth year students also lived at St. Henry's

During that first year of St. Henry's (1957-58), the third year students, which happened to be my class, were the "upper class" in the main building. Ron Schneider, one of my classmates, remembered, "We were called upon to be dorm prefects. Some of us were prefects over our own classmates and they took advantage of that. There was noise and play during grand silence. After one period, we were all fired in front of the entire student body, got a mark in conduct, and not allowed to be prefects again even in later years. Fourth year students came from St. Henry's to be prefects after that for two or three months at a time." I was not one of those fired but I do remember going from St. Henry's in my fourth year to be a dorm prefect for one assignment in the main dorm.

In my sixth year there was an experimental discipline inaugurated in which students reported on themselves to the rector for any infractions we made. The report was like an informal confession.

Visits, Letters, Vacations

Visits by parents and relatives were allowed during the time and hours appointed for that purpose. The first visiting day of the school year was the third Sunday in October.

We were warned that too frequent and unnecessary correspondence was an obstacle to progress in studies. Special Delivery letters or parcels could not be sent to us. We could not make or receive telephone calls, but necessary and urgent messages could be received for the students.

No student could subscribe to or receive newspapers or periodicals. One of my classmates, Edward Hahnenberg, convinced the seminary to subscribe to *America* for the library. Boxes containing provisions could not be sent or brought in.

The Rule allowed the Rector to open and read students' mail. John Doyle recalled this incident in early fall 1955, "one of our first year classmates was called into the big guy's office and told, as I heard later, that a bus was leaving in a few hours for, I believe, Traverse City and he was to be on It. The deal was he apparently had a girlfriend back home and she had been writing to him there at the Sem."

We were warned that vacation periods have particular dangers for youth. Faithful attention to religious duties was so necessary that no seminarian could hope to work out his vocation if he neglected them. Parents were expected to observe closely the association of their sons during vacation. They were to be mindful that from the time that their boys entered the Seminary, there were associations as well as forms of amusement, legitimate for young people in the world, that were unbecoming or even entirely forbidden to aspirants to the priesthood. The paganism of the theater, television, and modern literature was a positive danger. Every student was expected to assist at Holy Mass daily, if at all possible, and receive the Sacraments of Penance and the Eucharist as frequently as was the order of life in the Seminary.

In large measure, a seminarian was the responsibility of his Pastor with whom he was advised to keep in touch throughout the vacation. In accordance with statute No. 28 of the Second Synod of Grand Rapids, the Pastor was under obligation to submit to the Rector a signed and sealed report about the seminarian's conduct during vacation time.

Msgr. Falicki warned us about summer vacation at the end of the school year before heading home for vacation. In June 1957 he warned us not to abandon our vocation. He said we would always have the mark of being an ex-seminarian if we chose not to return. It reminds me of the Scarlet Letter by Nathaniel Hawthorne, except that the letter A would be a letter X stamped on my forehead for all to see. That was very shaming language and I carried it with me for years after I decided not to pursue my studies for the priesthood. John Doyle recalled Falicki saying, "a woman would consider it a feather in her cap to steal your vocation". These were his words of "direction" as we left for summer vacation.

Organized Activities

The daily routine, even study time, was carefully planned as one can readily see from the detailed schedule. There was little time for leisure and even that was usually organized or very short. The one exception was about an hour after the noon meal, still called dinner in those days. Our time for sports was compulsory recreation. Somehow those two words don't seem to fit together.

Various organizations and groups were part of seminary life but all were confined to the seminary. A mission society and the Newman Literary Society existed from the beginning. Reflecting the Polish heritage of many of the students, the "St. Stanislaus Literary Society was formed [in 1925] and presented a one-act comedy, *Mr. Kolasanty*, in Polish". [47]

The Rule in the 1950's referred to the areas of our lives outside study and chapel as "extra-curricular activities". Beginning in 1938, [48] these activities became "the responsibility of two student councils which carry the names of the College Students' Catholic Action Service and the High School Students' Catholic Action Service (SCAS). In each division, SCAS coordinated, under proper supervision and direction, the work of the various spiritual organizations and student committees for extra-curricular activities. All students were members and we elected our own officers. Meetings were held every Sunday morning as a medium for cultivating literary talent and extemporaneous speaking. The sessions also afforded pleasing and profitable diversion from the routine of the classroom. We gave speeches there and learned parliamentary procedure. When I was a student at St. Joe's from 1956-1961, the organizations and committees under the umbrella of SCAS were the following.

The Apostleship of Prayer promoted devotion to the Sacred Heart especially through the First Friday observance and the three degrees of membership.

The Archsodality of the Blessed Sacrament, an association founded by Blessed Peter Julian Eyrnard, fostered adoration to the Most Holy Sacrament and promoted the glory of Our Eucharistic Lord.

The Sodality of the Immaculate Conception of the Blessed Virgin Mary was a religious society, whose purpose was devotion to the Blessed Virgin as a means to a Christ-like life.

The Society of the Angelic Warfare was a confraternity canonically erected under the patronage of Our Blessed Lady and St. Thomas Aquinas. It was recommended by the Holy Father to seminarians as a most potent agency for purity.

The Academia, a Mission Society, sponsored an active membership in The Society for the Propagation of the Faith, mission study programs, prayers, and alms for the missions. Mission programs were presented at least once each month.

The Newman Literary Society afforded more extended opportunity for appreciation of literary arts and the application of the principles of rhetoric and public speaking. Debates, orations, declamations, reviews and criticism, and original essays formed the staples of the programs.

Students helped cut down trees

Other committees of SCAS were: St. Joseph's Committee for help in maintenance; the Committee on Community Affairs for recreational activities; the Committee on Democracy for the promotion of parliamentary procedure and patriotic programs; The Committee on Discussion Clubs (The Forum) for special work on various social questions; the Publicity Committee for the stimulation of interest in SCAS activities, The Athletic Committee for a program of sports; the Drama Committee for student skits and stage productions and the Latin Club.

23

In 1958 SCAS considered establishing a joint Board of Directors in meetings of the two houses and changing the SCAS constitution [49] but that didn't occur until 1962. [50] The last SCAS meeting was in September 1966. [51]

Orchestra and choir

In the fall of 1921 an orchestra was organized by Fr. Drinan. Fr. Hovorka took over as director after the first two performances. The orchestra had 3 first violins, 4 second violins, cello, bass, 2 cornets, saxophone, drums and piano and later two clarinets, flute and trombone. A viola was still needed. [52] The orchestra gave a concert at the Little Sisters of the Poor [53] auditorium in 1925. [54] A Junior Orchestra was being formed in 1924. By the time I enrolled in 1956, there was no orchestra or band. I had played French horn for two years and had hoped that I could continue.

The members of the Seminary Choir were selected from the music classes which all students attended. The choir prepared the Proprium de Tempore for Mass and Vespers of Sundays and Feast Days, and prepared a varied program of Masses and motets in modern polyphonic form when I was a student. In 1956 Fr. John Thome formed a 45 voice glee club. [55]

Student Newspaper

A student newspaper was started shortly after the move to the Burton site. The oldest copy I saw was February 1922. It was initially published every other month on one-sided legal paper stapled together and was called the *Prep Newsette*. News of sports activities were reported from the very beginning. A literary corner was added in 1924.[56] The newspaper changed to a monthly magazine in September 1924 [57] and was mimeographed on one-sided letter size paper and stapled together.

In October 1929 the name of the newspaper changed to *St. Joseph's Recorder*. [58] It was then printed on two sided 12"x21" paper and folded. The newspaper was discontinued in February 1933 but resumed in the fall 1938.

Each issue typically included sports news, jokes and stories about seminary life until 1947-1948 when "each issue had two parts, one the journalistic product of the high school, the other of the junior college.[59]" It became affiliated with the Catholic School Press Association on its 27th anniversary of publication in 1954. [60]

By this time an Alumni page was a feature of most issues and eight pages had become standard. In 1964 the *Recorder* was printed in a different process and had a new paper weight and type.[61] For this book my wife and I looked through every available issue in the archives at the Diocesan Center for Grand Rapids, Michigan.

My wife found this fascinating article in a 1925 issue and I just had to share it for a lighter moment:[62]

Rome Honors Our Rector Rt. Rev. Monsignor C.D. White, D.D.

Made Domestic Prelate to Our Holy Father

"A hundred hearts beat in jubilation, a hundred faces beam with joy, a hundred throats shout in exultation today, for out from the east, out from the seven hills of Rome where rose the sun this morning in a blaze of oriental pigmentation there has flashed across the waters a beam of papal splendor, and it now purples the large oak under whose spreading leafage we dwell.

"Our beloved Rector has been honored by the Chief of Christendom. From now on he will walk amongst us a purple-robed Monsignor. And no heart will swell with more genuine pride, no soul thrill with more unstinted joy, no tongue wax eloquent with more unfeigned praise, than those of his students who are wiser for his wisdom and more devoted for his unfailing example.

"So, we offer you, Right Reverend Rector, our unencompassed felicitations, exclaiming in loud and repeated accents: PROSIT!

"And we as fondly hope that in the very near future a day (should it not be an octave?) shorn of all page-chalk-pen-and-pencil-activity, will be called our own, whereon we may formally with high glee and festive function, usher our Right Reverend Monsignor into the honored row of the American prelacy."

I am adding a couple of names on the editorial staff that are of personal interest to me and perhaps to you too:

In 1943 Jeremiah Sullivan was editor; Francis Hackett and Kenneth Povish were on staff[63] and Dennis Wasco was a reporter in 1957-58.[64]

The High school staff for 1958-59 were: Editor Robert Walsh; Managing Editor Dennis Wasco; Art – Philip Frank; Sports – Thomas Rinkevich, Thomas Sullivan, James Runyan; Reporters – Thomas Schindler, Thomas Doud, Walter Broad, Thomas Platte; Typist – Paul Kress. [65]

Sports

Sports were well established early. In 1924-25 the Bulletin reported there were a football field, baseball field, tennis courts, and handball courts. Students were required to participate. The 1962 *Bulletin* said this about athletics and leisure: "

The spacious grounds of the Seminary furnished ample room for athletics. Baseball, tennis, handball, football, softball, and skating provide healthful outdoor recreation for the students. The gymnasium and. recreation room have facilities for indoor leisure time activities; such as basketball, table tennis, and radio programs.

Guys playing football 1956

Boys playing handball on an outdoor court

In 1928 Mr. Whalen donated eight acres of land west of Galewood, where a new ball field was established. [66] In 1927, an experimental golf course was created with a real course created in 1928. [67] Could it have been created on the Whalen donation?

In 1931, six new handball courts were built behind the new garage. [68] In the summer of 1940 two new horseshoe courts were constructed. [69]

There was a gym in the main building from the beginning. It was also used as a theatre and auditorium for special programs such as orations and debates. In addition there was a recreation room in the basement of the main building in which one could participate in various leisure activities. The room and the activities changed over the years.

The Activities Building was constructed in1955-56 opening for use in the fall of 1956 with three regulation size basketball courts and four indoor handball courts. It also had lockers, showers, and a director's office.

Four boys playing handball in new indoor court

I do not know how sports were organized, if at all, prior to 1938 when the Athletic Committee was formed under SCAS. Its duties were to arrange for sporting events. All students were assigned to football teams in the fall, basketball teams in the winter and baseball teams in the spring. All games were intramural. SCAS also organized Field Day events. The seminary newspaper reported on the sports in every issue from the beginning.

When we were not involved in organized team play, we could participate in handball, tennis, bowling before 1940, table tennis, and pick-up games of football, baseball when the weather permitted, or basketball.

There were special games from time to time. In 1942 the students defeated the clergy in a pass-touch football game, 13-6.[70] In 1943 the clergy upset an all-star student team in a football game, 12-6.[71] In 1944 students defeated alumni from St. Mary's Baltimore in basketball, 64-16. Chester Pilarski (Fr. Chet died in 2015) scored 25 points and Mikulski scored 18 for St. Joseph.[72]

Boys playing basketball

There were bowling lanes in the basement of the main building for a number of the early years.

Hockey was a popular sport on our own ice rink until about the 1950's when it was banned because it was considered to be too violent. There was still an ice rink created every winter and skating was very popular. I tried it a few times but preferred to play handball on the indoor courts.

In 1940 the ice rink was in good shape and hockey games were being played [73] but in 1955 and 1956, the seminary held an ice carnival with various events and contests for skaters.[74]

Jim Beckstrom, a classmate, recalled this about ice skating and the ice carnivals:

"I certainly do very fondly remember the ice skating rink and the Ice Carnivals. I had learned to skate very young, Dad was quite athletic, I started with a pair of adult skates over my high-top shoes, so had quite the ankle support. I inherited his skates when I went to St Joes.

"There was a "giant" roller, about 3 feet in diameter and 6-8 feet long - we used that to pack the first snowfall down to begin the rink making process. A 2-3 inch diameter fire hose supplied the water for creating and maintaining the ice. After each day's skating, not having a Zamboni, everyone grabbed a shovel and we scraped the loose stuff off so the rink could be resurfaced. Slave labor, but win-win - we enjoyed many days of great skating.

"A few of the games we played: an ice skating version of "capture the flag". The flag was a skate blade protector, and it was placed on the ice with a gentlemen's agreement of a 3 foot diameter safe zone where an opponent could get into to stay until an opportune moment for grabbing the flag and skating back to his team's side of the rink before someone from the other team captured his team's flag. I don't remember

what happened to an opponent who was tagged by the goalie before he got into the safe zone.

Boys skating on our home made rink

"*A second one was even more fun. One person was "it", stood in the center, and everyone else was over on one side. When "it" called, everyone skated to the other side, and "it" tried to tag as many guys as he could. Repeat, everyone tagged stayed in the middle, so it was cumulative, eventually there was just Mike and me not yet caught. Mike cheated, he was on figure skates, so he had a maneuvering advantage <grin>.*

"*A third ice skating events was the train race. A train was one guy standing, leaning forward, a second in a sitting position with his hands on the standing guy's skates, and the standing guy's hands on the sitting guy's knees. The third guy was the engine, he pushed the first two. I think the race course was a round trip straight down and back the longer direction of the rink. Again, Mike W. is in my memory as the fellow blue who did the best since he used figure skates, because they have notches in the toes of the blades. The rest of the races that I remember were 2 and 4 lap races, both clockwise and counter-clockwise, plus one counter-clockwise backwards.*"

29

Orations and Debates

As part of the public speaking curriculum and under the umbrella of the Newman Literary Society, sixth year students participated in giving orations and participating in a formal debate. Senior Orations were started in 1921 in the spring before graduation. Debates most likely started at the beginning of the seminary. The *Prep Newsette* reported that the annual debates were scheduled in March 1925.

Some of the debate topics were:

In 1939 students debated whether chain stores should be curbed and whether tipping should be abolished. [75]

In 1940 students debated whether all electric utilities should be governmentally owned and operated. Other debates were about maximum hours and minimum wages and consumers' cooperatives.[76] Electric utilities debate was defeated and the debate for minimum wages, maximum hours was defeated. [77]

In 1941 debaters claimed that Dies Committee has done more harm than good; In the present conflict, the United States shall not aid Great Britain; and that the United States and Canada ought to complete the Great Lakes-St. Lawrence Waterway. The negative teams won all three. [78]

In 1942 Federal control of the press and Pan American Union were debate topics. Negative teams won both. [79]

In 1943 the negative team won in the debate of right of labor to strike in defense work.[80]

In 1944 General sales tax proponents gained the decision over the opposition in an interesting senior debate. The negative team won the debate "Resolved that the federal system of restricting agricultural production be discontinued." [81]

In 1945 the affirmative team won the debate on socialized medicine. [82]

In 1947 students debated that Congress enact legislation providing for compulsory arbitration in all labor disputes; that the Security Council of the United Nations control the use of atomic energy; that the federal government solve the housing problem; that the United States should officially oppose the system of cartels in the future international economic council.[83]

The 1948 topics included reduction of national taxation, American aid to Europe and universal military training. [84]

The 1951 debates involved neutrality of Germany in the present crises, what stand is the United States to take in the present world situation and televising football games. [85]

Interestingly the 1952 debate topics were secret until debated. [86]

Students in 1953 debated cutting federal spending and that wage and price controls be taken out of the hands of government. [87]

In 1954 students debated that federal taxes be reduced and that the annual wage be adopted by industry. [88]

In 1955 debaters argued that Michigan ought to enact a minimum wage law. Other topics included bingo and lotteries; public and private control of utilities; and that a maximum speed law be adopted in Michigan. [89]

In 1957 debate topics were: That the Federal government control air traffic adequately (affirmative side won unanimously); That games of chance be abolished as a means of Church support (judges voted for negative, students for affirmative); That the testing of hydrogen bombs be stopped (judges voted for negative, students for affirmative); That college students engaged in competitive sports be subsidized (negative team won); That the Suez agreement of October 19, 1954, before Nasser's nationalization, be changed (debate had not occurred at press time). [90]

In 1958 there was a two man debate on capital punishment in Michigan (Judges and High School voted affirmative and College voted negative). [91]

In 1959 one of the debate topics was whether Hawaii should be admitted to the union. [92] Other debate topics were: whether nuclear tests should be banned; whether the 3% sales tax in Michigan should be abolished; whether Braceros should be banned from the United States; whether racketeering should be rooted out of the unions by the federal government; whether the government should support the basic commodities at 90% of parity. [93]

Debate topics in 1960 were: That the United States should increase trade with Russia; that the vernacular be used in the Holy Mass except for the Canon; that laws forbidding hitchhiking be made, where they are not made, and strictly enforced in all states of the United States; that teenagers be tried in law courts as adults. [94]

In 1961 there were two articles in the *St. Joseph's Recorder* about the orations and debates. Since this was my class I include them both here in full. [95]

> *The time-honored tradition of sixth class debates began this year on January 1; with a topic which has concerned many great minds and is of immediate interest to many of our seminarians: "Resolved that all government aid to agriculture be gradually eliminated." Upholding the resolution were Myron Hawkins and James Swiat; opposing were Robert Lesinski and Thomas Popma. In an extremely close voting-a compliment to the ability of both teams, the students voted affirmative, the judges, negative. The second debate, which noticeably interested the students, centered on the resolution: "Resolved that the United States government should subsidize its amateur athletes for competition in the Olympic Games." The affirmative team was composed of Edward Hahnenberg and Gerald Willing; the negative of James Beckstrom and Francis Fallon. Despite strong presentations by both sides, both the*

judges and students sided with the affirmative, on the basis of their outstanding constructive speeches.

In a single debate on Feb. 5, Thomas Schindler maintained, while Robert Tisch opposed the resolution "Resolved that all our armed forces be consolidated into a single fighting force under, one head." Both debaters organized and presented the material well, but influenced perhaps by a fine negative rebuttal, both students and judges favored the negative.

The fourth debate was held on Saturday evening, Feb. 11, because of a conflict in the schedule. The subject was: "Resolved that government aid be given to non-public schools on the same basis as to public schools." On the affirmative side were Norbert Bufka and Kent Lewis; on the negative, John Mullally and Ronald Schneider. The issue was complicated (with some digressions) as was reflected in the balloting: the Judges voted for the affirmative, the students for the negative.

In weeks to come diplomatic relations with Cuba and the propriety of athletic scholarships will be the subjects of debate. We congratulate those debaters who have already met the test on their excellent performance and encourage those yet to meet in battle to maintain these standards.

Several steps have been taken to make this year's debates more enjoyable and profitable to all. A loud- speaker has been employed to ensure that all can hear everything that is said, and the debates have been recorded to enable the debaters to get an accurate idea of their own performance. In addition, the chairmen have done an excellent job in explaining the principles of debate to the younger members of the community, particularly by employing realistic allegories. As in past years the debates have been held after Vespers to enable Msgr. Martin to attend and also to provide more time for the debate and the judging.

The debate season entered its final phase, after a two-week pause, on February 26, when William Birchmeier and Paul Kress, on the affirmative, and Thomas Polzin and Thomas Rinkevich, on the negative, argued the resolution: "Resolved that all diplomatic relations with Cuba should be severed." Although such a step had already been taken by our government, the issue was still very controversial, as it appeared from the debate. Both judges and students sided with the affirmative on the basis of their more forceful presentation.

The subject of the final debate, on March 5, was: "Resolved that the granting of athletic scholarships should be discontinued in American colleges and universities." In this single debate, Clark Hurlbert upheld the resolution, while Robert Walsh opposed it. The latter, by his excellent delivery and well directed arguments, won the decision of both students and judges.

And so ended the sixth-class debates for one more year. As the chairmen laid aside their well-worn analogies, and the judges ripped up their ballot sheets, and students forgot their impassioned questions, another time-honored tradition was carried on with the beginning of the sixth-class orations.

March 12 saw the first of this year's orations, as Dennis Wasco led off with an excellent presentation of the life and work of Dr. Thomas Dooley, "The Splendid American." The labors and hopes of the Spanish Apostolate formed the basis of Myron Hawkins' very timely oration. Thomas Popma followed with a very practical and worthwhile discussion of the heart and our physical health. The final oration of the day was presented by James Swiat, who ably explained the Moral Rearmament Movement and its significance for Catholics.

Robert Lesinski started the second group of orations, on March 26, with a soul-stirring portrayal of the life of a camp counsellor. "The Motherly Face of Materialism" was the subject of Edward Hahnenberg's very thoughtful and pertinent oration. James Beckstrom then analyzed the present situation in "Berlin - The City Where East Meets West." Gerald Willing, the last speaker of the morning, explained the detailed training that goes to make a man a Communist.

The third set of orations was presented on April 16;. "Africa's Challenge to the Free World" was the topic of Frank Fallon's informative analysis. The dangers and implications of psychological advertising were very forcefully described by Thomas Schindler. Robert Tisch spoke on the fate of the buffalo, "The Monarch of the Plains", and the conservation of our natural resources. To end the program, Norbert Bufka expounded on the importance of understanding the Protestant Reformation in convert-making.

Debate topics in 1962 were: that the first six grades of elementary school be dropped from the Catholic school system; that the president of the United States be elected by the direct vote of the people; that Congress should repeal the exemptions of the unions under the anti-trust acts.[96]

In 1963 the debate topics were: that the United States should withdraw from the United Nations; that the sales tax on food and medicine be withdrawn in the state of Michigan; that government scholarships be awarded to qualified high school graduates; that the constitution proposed for the state of Michigan be adopted.[97]

Even though we were isolated from much of what was happening outside our walls and restricted in our connection with that world, students still had a grasp on that reality in these debates and orations. Many of those debate topics were forward thinking while others were caught in the old ways of thinking. Some topics are still being debated today.

Drama Club

Students performed many plays over the history of St. Joseph's Seminary. I certainly don't have a listing of all of them but I did find a consistent pattern of offering a play around the time of Halloween, Christmas, and May 1. The Christmas play became an annual tradition quite early and continued through most of the seminary's history. Below are a few examples followed by a list of the Christmas presentations.

A one act play, *The Great Pumpkin Case*, was presented in the fall of 1923.[98]. This was before Charlie Brown! In 1945 "Theater Guild put on two plays: *Ecce Homo*, the passion play, and *There'll Be A Hot Time In The Old Home Tonight*, the annual entertainment for the Little Sisters of the Poor." [99]

In the winter of 1951 students performed *The Student Prince*[100] and *The Mikado* in 1952. [101] In 1957 the Drama Committee presented *Crime Conscious*. [102]

In 1958 a minstrel show was presented on May 1st, feast day of St. Joseph the Worker.[103] An adaptation of *My Fair Lady*, called *My Fair Laddie*" was presented in the spring of 1959. [104] *The Spooky Tavern* was the Halloween drama in 1959. [105] A year later the Halloween drama was *Vengeance of Buddha*.[106] The May 1961 musical was an adaptation of *No Time For Sergeants*.[107]

The Halloween 1961 play was *No Curtain Calls*.[108]

Between Christmas and Lent 1962 a modern abstract drama, *Lucifer at Large*, was presented.[109] A few months later, the May 1st musical was *The Uncle Sam Story*. [110]

In the 1962-63 school year, *Lucifer's Lodge* was the Halloween production [111] and the pre-Lenten play was *Storm Over Nuevaluz*.[112]

The Music Man was the May 1963 production.[113]

In the 1964-65 school year *A message from Khufu* was the Halloween play [114]and the May 1, 1965 musical was a vaudeville show. [115]

The presentation of a Christmas drama began in 1922. There was none in 1937 and 1938. [116]

1925: *Hermigild*, a Spanish drama [117]
1926: *St. Francis* [118]
1927: *Domitian, the End of the Flavians* [119]
1928: *Hearts of Gold* [120]
1929: *Men of St. Quentin* [121]
1930: *The Hidden Gem*[122]
1931: *If I Were a King* [123]

1932: *The Merchant of Venice* [124]
1939: *Mysteries of the Mass*[125]
1940: *Monsignor's Hour*[126]
1942: *Brother Orchid* [127]
1943: *Old Wang*, a Chinese play [128]
1944: *Career Angel* [129]
1945: *Knight's Lodging* [130]
1947: *Brother Petroc's Return* [131]
1948: *Through the Eye of a Needle* [132]
1949: *The Victim of the Seal* [133]
1951: *Harvey* [134]
1952: *Nothing But The Truth* [135]
1953: *Flight of the Gull* [136]
1954: *Cox and Box* [137]
1955: *Knight's Lodging* [138]
1956: *The Billion Dollar Saint* with St. Francis of Assisi as the title character [139]
1957 *Arsenic and Old Lace* [140]
1959 *Brother Orchid* [141]
1960 *Mikado* [142]
1961 *Yeomen of the Guard* [143]
1962 *H.M.S. Pinafore* [144]
1964 *Shepherds on the Shelf* [145]
1965 *Visit to a Small Planet* [146]

Ordinary events
Even the everyday activities of life were directed by seminary rules.

Laundry
We didn't do our own laundry nor did the sisters take care of that. Our moms did our laundry. In preparation for coming to the seminary one of the items needed was a box in which to send our laundry home each week for cleaning. These were sturdy boxes, I presume made of durable plastic or metal. They were picked up each Saturday and returned on Saturday in the cortile.

Fr. Dennis Morrow recalled, "The cortile was that outdoor semi-enclosed area between the chapel and the west wing. It had a tile roof and glazed brick construction, and was handy if you wanted to step outdoors for a breath of fresh air even if it was pouring rain. You could look down into it from the restrooms on the first floor next to the study hall.

The cortile in 1925

It was like a big, 3-sided porch. We made ample use of it in nicer weather to step outside from the basement locker room and shine our shoes. On Saturday mornings, the pickup and delivery of laundry kits by local car-pooling parents would take place there while we were in class. The pickup was supervised, I believe, by a couple of upper classmen. The rest of us were to be occupied so that we would not be able to visit with family members. We had visiting days to do that. There were similarities between Burton Street and the county jail, but our motivation for being there was different!" Laundry boxes traveled by mail for the students who did not live in the Grand Rapids area.

John Doyle recalled, "It would seem that any mail that came in via the Post Office was read by someone in authority. It didn't happen to me because all my mail came by way of the laundry case dropped off each Saturday morning by someone in my family. I was lucky to be from Grand Rapids." This type of mail delivery, of course, was a violation of the rules. I am almost surprised his kit wasn't opened and inspected!

Haircuts

Instead of the students going to the barber, he came to us. In 1926 Mr. Millard had been the Seminary barber since the institution was started in 1909 and continued to come every Saturday despite having his own manufacturing business. [147]

In 1930 the barber shop was moved from the basement to the science room along with a new barber chair [148] so the basement room could be used as a radio room. I believe the barber shop was moved back to the basement by the time I was a student there in the 1950's.

In 1944 "The barber's assistant this year was Albert Watson. In former years the barber was prevented from shaving students' faces. Now he is also prevented from shaving their heads, for G.I. haircuts are banned by our Rector."[149] The barber was Al Skryzala from 1945 to at least 1955.[150]

Sickness

There was an infirmary in the main building which generally had enough beds to care for those with illness. Sr. Christopher, a registered nurse, served in the infirmary from 1936 [151] to the mid-1960's. There were a few flu outbreaks over the years.

In February 1930, a significant number of students were ill, keeping the infirmary full. [152]

In 1944, flu cases filled the infirmary the first week of February. [153] Later in 1944 "on the last Sunday of October, 44 students were in the infirmary." [154]

In March 1947, only 12 were sick in the infirmary. [155] In February 1955 flu struck the seminary for the second time after an outbreak at Christmas.[156]

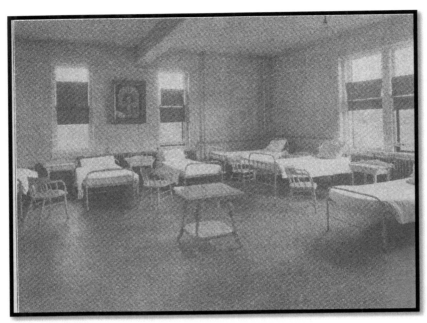

The Infirmary on the Second Floor in 1925

Dennis LaFave recalled his bout with the flu in late spring 1957: "I was the first one to get the Asian flu and ended up at St Mary's Hospital for a week. I was then sent home for two weeks over the objections of Msgr Fallicky. When i came back, everyone was sick. I was so far behind that I could not pass finals. That ended my career at the seminary."

There were over 100 cases of the flu the week of October 13, 1957. [157] I remember another flu incident in the following year. There were so many of us sick they sent us all to our rooms where I remember playing cards with Doug Hogan that day. Not many of us were very sick.

Jim Beckstrom recalled this incident in the infirmary: "I had the mumps and was confined to the infirmary. Steve VanderClay smuggled sci-fi books in for me to read. He somehow locked himself out and Msgr. Shaw had to unlock the room for him after which Msgr. Shaw chastised him."

Leisure time

In 1922 editors of the *Newsette* encouraged discussion about getting a Victrola. [158] In 1923, the seminary purchased a moving picture and stereopticon machine with donated funds. [159] In 1931 "A Howard super-heterodyne radio was installed in the gymnasium." [160] It is important to keep in mind that these objects were the high tech devices of their day.

While the following article is not entirely clear to me, it does tell us the importance of a radio for entertainment in the 1930's.

"In its Paleolithic era the small basement room was a mute witness to the dire deeds of the barber's shears. After a few years the barber chair – and the barber – was moved up a flight of stairs and the old "barbershop" was converted into a sort of locker room. Comes 1938 and another change occurs in the room's humble existence. Compartments removed, expert hands soon changed the walls to a more cheery color. A table and chairs were unearthed. Such was the birth of the Radio Room, where we gather of Saturday afternoons to listen to Notre Dame march to victory. The radio has at last found a resting place for its weary tubes. Requiescat in pace!" [161]

In several articles in the 1940's we learn of the birth of a recreation room and what it contained:

In the 1939-1940 school year, *"A new recreation room has been provided for the students' use. The stage, transformed by the removal of scenery, provides ample space for indoor recreation. Here have been installed ping pong tables, card tables and a sturdy piano. Transformation has also been effected in the bowling alley room where shuffle board courts have been installed along the side of the alleys."* [162]

"The bowling alleys, long a part of the Seminary recreation equipment, have been judged obsolete, and the space is being converted into a large recreation room. The new hall will have ping pong tables, a radio and accommodations for games. Other plans are being worked out by the Community Affairs committee. At present a contest is being conducted to select a suitable name for the room." The room opened on Feb 21 [1946] and was called 'DEN'". [163]

"On the night of the Christmas party, December 20, [1946], we heard a startling announcement to the effect that immediately after the party all would remain assembled in the "Den" for (believe it or not) movies. This entertainment consisted of short selections of news, sports, and also a cartoon." [164]

In early 1959 A Hi-Fi Committee was established to encourage music appreciation with listening sessions on Saturday night and Sunday afternoons in St. Henry's Hall. Committee was: Cwik, Hirsch, Sigmund, Smolinski, Hahnenberg and Hawkins. [165]

In early 1962 a darkroom was installed on the third floor of St. Henry's. [166]

Odds 'n Ends

In 1922, someone asked the question, "Why is it that the Sem dairy which was to be kept up by a member of the fifth or sixth class has been discontinued since Feb 7, 1921?" [167]

Apparently there was a pet at the seminary, for in 1923, the faithful cat Topsy died and was replaced by the dog Milly. [168] Of course this is quite believable because 600 Burton Street was still in a rural area.

Apparently newly ordained priests had to return to the seminary for post ordination studies and exams.

On Tuesday, May 9, 1922 the Junior Clergy had their second examination [169] and in 1925 Junior Clergy of the diocese wrote their annual examinations on Theology and Canon Law on May 2. [170]

In 1943 during World War II 25 upper classmen were certified as air raid wardens. [171]

Fr. James Moran and Fr. Charles Salatka were ordained on February 24, 1945 in the seminary chapel. [172] Fr. Moran later became Rector of the seminary and Fr. Salatka became bishop of Marquette, Michigan.

George Fulk, Class of 1961, recalled in a letter to Bob Lesinski in 1973, this incident in the physics classroom.

"Remember the time that Bob Lesinski went down into the utility crawl space in the floor of the Physics classroom just as Belardo came in? Tom Popma (or John Mullally?) put the cover over the hole with Bob inside, then I set my chair on top so Bob could not get out. Bob called 'let me out', for most of the class. Poor Belardo could not figure out where that muffled sound was coming from. My sides ached from suppressed laughter." Bellardo was John Bellardo, the teacher.

Chemistry Class

My Class of 1961 was kind of a rebel class in some ways reflected perhaps by another incident in Mr. Bellardo's chemistry class that John Mullally recalled this way:

"Tom Popma and Bob Lesinski finished their chemistry lab work early and were killing time. Tom thought they could make a gas flame thrower by putting a two holed rubber stopper into a gallon jug. One hole would

lead to the gas jet, the other hole to a straight glass tube. They did this, turned on the gas to fill the gallon jug with gas, then lit the gas coming out of the straight tube pointing to the ceiling. Tom told me he saw a nice flame coming out of the tube.

"When Mr. 'Jeb' Belardo turned his back to the class to write on the now vanished blackboard, they would light the flame-thrower to the giggles of all. The flame would nearly reach the ceiling. They would turn off the gas as he slowly turned to face the class. I believe it was the third attempt at this ha-ha moment that the flame disappeared into the tube and the glass gallon jug exploded, throwing glass shards all over the place. Mr. Bellardo's grossly understated question, "Aba, aba, who's been playing with the sulfa?" was our class greeting to each other for a long time.

"Tom's hand, which was close to the glass jug, was badly cut and he had to go to the hospital to be sewed up. Some of the tendons in his hand were cut, but it all healed up pretty well. Bob had glass shards shot into his stomach.

"The glass doors of the cabinets containing all the other chemicals were shattered along with some chemical bottles inside. Thank God or St. Joseph that there was not a secondary explosion when all these chemicals intermixed. I remember Bob L and the other culprits got 2 marks in conduct for nearly killing all of us!

"Every tragedy has a lesson to learn. 100% methane is not explosive. The methane in the glass jug did not explode the first two times because there was 100% methane in the jug. However, in the boom time they must have held the match to the tubing before they turn on the gas. When the proper ratio of methane to oxygen was reached: BOOM

"Our class dodged a possibly fatal encounter of the worst kind. I was not injured."

Chuck Neubecker added that he was across from Bob and Tom at the same lab table and received shards of glass as well. Both Bob and Chuck were treated in the emergency room and released. The fourth lab partner is unknown but possibly Bob Walsh.

By the fall of 1960, after 16 years of teaching at the seminary, Mr. Bellardo left the seminary faculty to work in the labs at Aquinas College.[173] I am guessing this was an involuntary departure quite possibly related to the flamethrower incident.

Holidays and Free Days

When I was a student at St. Joseph's Seminary, students could go home for Thanksgiving, Christmas, and Easter. This was not always the case.

In 1923 the Seminary Military Band was featured in the Thanksgiving celebration. [174] In 1924 Thanksgiving Day was celebrated with music by the orchestra and recitations by students. A big turkey dinner was served. [175]

By 1940 students were allowed to leave the campus on Thanksgiving Day, "City students and those residing within a forty mile radius left for their respective homes at 8:00 am on Thanksgiving Day. The rest of the students amused themselves at the Seminary in the morning. In the afternoon they were permitted to visit various points of interest in the city. All returned at 4:30 p.m."[176]

In 1940 students stayed at the seminary during Holy Week but did not have classes. Easter Monday was a free day.[177] In 1945 students were granted Easter vacation for the first time. [178]

Guys hanging out during free time April 1957

A "free day" was one in which there were no classes. The schedule was similar to Sunday but there was not always a Solemn High Mass like on Sunday and Holy Days. These free days were greatly enjoyed and much appreciated by the students who worked hard at their studies most of the time. Some free days were scheduled in the calendar but others came unexpectedly.

On the occasional days when there were no classes and no mass, recreation extended from breakfast until dinner. The afternoon was free until study was resumed at 5:30.

In 1953 a free day was given to commemorate the anniversary of the coronation of Pope Pius XII[179] and a free day was given on Saturday, October 10, to honor the Rt. Rev. Msgr. Shaw and Very Rev. Msgr. Verreau on their elevation to their respective positions.[180]

In 1954 students got a free day to celebrate Most Rev. Allen Babcock as Bishop of Grand Rapids. [181]

Prayer

Prayer was one of the most important aspects of seminary life. It was routinely built into the schedule. It was believed that if a person was directed to pray regularly then that practice would become a habit.

The daily routine included several times when we went to the chapel to pray. The first thing we did after getting up and dressed in the morning was go to chapel for morning prayer, private meditation, mass and spiritual reading. In the middle of the day we made a visit to the Blessed Sacrament in the chapel. Since the teaching of the Catholic Church is that Jesus is truly present in the consecrated host, or rather that the consecrated host is Jesus, much attention was given to reverence it and adore it. This daily devotion was short and reinforced that belief.

At the end of the semester from Saturday to Monday we participated in Forty Hours Devotion to the Blessed Sacrament, a devotion established in the eleventh century. It concluded with special prayers and reposition of the Blessed Sacrament in the tabernacle. Many neighboring priests would come for this final service which generally ended with a festive meal.

Towards evening we prayed the rosary together, listened to some spiritual reading, and said night prayers.

A rosary is a repetitive prayer of decades during which the person meditates on a mystery of faith, such as the Resurrection of Jesus. A decade consists of one Our Father, ten Hail Marys and one Glory Be. Praying the rosary meant some introductory prayers and then five of these decades. A full rosary was fifteen decades involving Joyful, Sorrowful, and Glorious mysteries of our faith. Pope John Paul II added another five called the Luminous mysteries. To keep track of the prayers said, a rosary of beads was often used but fingers work pretty well also.

We had a prayer book designed for use by students of this seminary. One was prepared in 1928 [182]and I believe that was the same one we used in the 1950's. Many of the prayers were in Latin but some were in English. The prayers before and after meals were in Latin but we prayed the rosary in English although the prayers were in our prayer book in Latin.

In order to maintain a more respectful atmosphere during Holy Week, [183] from Thursday until Saturday, students were summoned by a clapper, not by electronic bells.[184]

On Tuesday of the third week in September we began our annual retreat. This was marked by the painful rule of silence during the whole time other than talking with a priest about my spiritual life. There was no talking at meal times or on walks around the campus or at any other time until the retreat was over on Saturday. The retreat was filled with talks, called conferences, by various priests about a variety of subjects during those few days.

The Day of Recollection was observed on the first Sunday of each month. This was like a mini-retreat with this schedule:

9: 15 - Solemn .Mass and Exposition of the Blessed Sacrament

11:00 - Conference

12:15 - Rosary

12:30 - Dinner

2:00 - Conference

3:00 - Vespers and Reposition of Blessed Sacrament

Solemn High Mass, usually with a sermon, was celebrated on every Sunday and on all the Holy Days as well as the Feast Days of St. Joseph, Patron of the Seminary, The Annunciation, St. Thomas Aquinas (March 7), Purification (February 2), anniversary of the coronation of Pope Pius XII (March 12), anniversary of the consecration of Bishop Babcock of Grand Rapids Diocese (March 25), and Ash Wednesday. This Mass was at 9:15 a.m. A Solemn High Mass includes a lot of singing and Gregorian chant. A low Mass is merely read or recited without music or singing and was the Mass before breakfast.

The Saturday Benediction was at 8:40 a.m.

The Way of the Cross was prayed during Lent on Wednesday, 5:00 p.m. and Friday, 6:15 p.m.

In 1944, "Numerous students were disillusioned recently when Fr. Shaw committed his first recorded error before the student body. Known for having the Seminary routine "down cold", Father startled the student body recently when he started the afternoon study period with the recitation of the Angelus instead of the usual prayer." [185]

Changes began taking shape

The 1950's saw the beginning of a widespread social and cultural shift in the United States and indeed much of the world. One aspect of this shift was rock and roll music but the shift expanded in many directions in the 1960's. We witnessed the sexual revolution of free love, hippie communes, and Woodstock. We witnessed the rise of the war in Vietnam and protests of the war with the shootings at Kent State. We also saw the assassinations of prominent public figures: John F. Kennedy, Dr. Martin Luther King, Jr. and Robert F. Kennedy. The civil rights movement began, resulting in historic laws against segregation and discrimination.

The Roman Catholic Church was not exempt from change either. In 1958 Cardinal Giuseppe Roncalli was elected Pope, taking the name John XXIII. Within a short period of time he called for an ecumenical council of all the Roman Catholic bishops of the world to be held at the Vatican. This meeting was called the Second Vatican Council or simply Vatican II. The First Vatican Council took place in 1870 and declared the very controversial doctrine of papal infallibility. This new council was to be very different since it was called to open the windows of the Church and get some fresh air into its life. Pope John called it aggiornamento. He called the church to embrace the modern world rather than condemn it. It was the first council in the history of the Christian Church to be called to be pro-active rather than defensive and condemning heresies. The council met from 1962 to 1965. Pope Francis has declared that we have not yet begun to implement Vatican II.

In 1957 St. Joseph's Seminary began to change as well with the appointment of Fr. James P. Moran as rector to replace the strict rule of Msgr. Falicki. Fr. Moran recognized the changing times. A supplement to the Rule was established to meet the changing situation of St. Henry's Hall where the upper classmen resided. See Appendix A for the complete Rule and supplement. One very simple change gave permission for the upper classmen to smoke in a designated place and time. Today we might find this foolish but at that time the danger of smoking was not yet fully known. As I recall all but three of my classmates in the last year had not smoked. I was one of them. I changed that on our fun day away from the seminary in the last month before graduation. This fun day was an annual event for upcoming graduates. I smoked a full pack of Newports! I didn't feel very good the next day.

George Fulk recalled his experience with smoking at that time:

"My dad sent me a pack of BIGGER HAIR. We were in the 4th year and now it was ok to smoke on the path behind St. Henry's Hall. Everyone was smoking a pipe and I wanted to too but did not have tobacco. So I asked my dad to send some. He sent BIGGER HAIR, a big pack of it. I smoked it and turned green. I felt so sick for the rest of the day that JP saw me and called me into his office. I told him I was sick from smoking some tobacco my dad sent. He asked me to show it to him. I did, thinking it was just some regular stuff. JP almost smiled when he saw it. It took me a long time to figure out why my dad sent this terrible stuff. He hoped I'd get sick and not want to smoke. Dad was a heavy smoker himself." J. P. was Fr. James P. Moran, the rector.

Another change was the lifting of the requirement for compulsory recreation and the assignment of all students to teams.

Msgr. Falicki held the first open house in the fall of 1956 to show off the new Activities Building. On October 19,1958 the main attractions were the new kitchen and dining facilities and the chapel addition.[186] In 1959 2,000 people attended the 4th Open House. [187]The number of visitors in 1960 was 1,200.[188] In 1961 that number was nearly the same at 1,100.[189] The open house was a way to thank the many people who donated to the building program but also an opportunity to acquaint people with life at the seminary.

The rising enrollment at St. Joseph's over nearly two decades probably had some influence on the decision by Bishop Woznicki of Saginaw to build a seminary there. Many of the Saginaw boys who wanted to go to the seminary had been going to St. Joseph's. The dramatic increase in enrollment at St. Joseph's continued at St. Paul's in Saginaw but also was part of the reason for the reduction in enrollment at St. Joseph's

St. Paul's Seminary in Saginaw opened on September 12, 1961 with 82 students. In 1963 it had 159 students (145 in high school and 14 in college).[190]

Dramatic changes took place in the 1960's at St. Joe's in prayer and socialization of students. The faculty and students were very much aware of the proceedings and documents of Vatican II. Msgr. Shaw led the recitation of the rosary every Friday night praying for the success of Vatican II.

Discussion groups were organized among the students with faculty members serving as moderators. Among the topics discussed were "seminary life, the Mass and Vatican Council II" [191] and the "changes called for by Vatican II". [192]

Beginning in 1964, students from St. Joe's participated in an Inter-Seminary Conference with others from Michigan to discuss the future of seminaries and how they are set up. Several participants from Protestant divinity schools attended as well. [193]

Prayer

On December 4, 1963 Pope Paul VI promulgated the first document of Vatican II, *Sacrosanctum concilium* (*Constitution on the Liturgy*), calling for a transformation of the liturgy and the way we pray publicly in our sacraments and Mass. The faculty and student at St. Joseph's began implementing changes very quickly. Some of them were:

In early 1964 "Lenten Scripture Service with a great deal of student participation replaced the usual Friday Way of the Cross service." [194]

In 1964-65 prayers were said in English every other day, alternating with Latin, instead of all being in Latin as was the practice when I was there. By the fall of 1964 some prayers had been re-written in modern English. On

Sunday there was one Mass instead of two. [195] Mass facing the people was celebrated for the first time on December 6, 1964. [196]

In the fall of 1965 senior students began "celebrating Mass in Room 4 at St. Henry's with students very involved in the preparation of the liturgy and environment. The celebrations have reawakened a sense of community among the students and faculty who join them." [197]

Sports

In 1963-64 "Mr. Don Lennon joins staff as part-time coach, teaching fundamentals of different sports." [198] This may suggest a greater emphasis on sports but on May 12, 1965 "Field Day changed to Orientation Day with sports being dropped. It was a chance to introduce young men to the seminary." [199]

In the spring of 1969 the clergy defeated the students in a softball game 19-9. [200]

John Andrusiak, a student in 1974-75, said there were interscholastic sports with several schools in the area.

Recruitment

In the mid 1960's seminarians were involved in recruitment, meeting with prospective students and their families [201] and went out to local Catholic schools to talk about seminary life. [202]

Outreach

Students tutored in the cathedral reading program, college students taught CCD classes at local parishes, and eight students taught religion to children with developmental disabilities at St. Francis School. [203]

It was reported in the *Recorder* that 14 seminarians along with Fr. Ancona joined the march in Selma on March 14, 1965 [204] but in 2015 Msgr. Ancona says this event did not happen.

Socialization

In the spring of 1965 sophomores and juniors visited the Museum of Science and Industry in Chicago [205] and the fourth class visited Greenfield Village. [206] Since the report on the march to Selma was false, I wonder if this one was a well.

In the year 1965-66 40 students attended a New Christy Minstrels concert at Calvin College. [207] In 1966 150 people attended Hootenanny Halloween. Some of the performers were young women. [208] In the fall of 1968 St. Henry's hosted a college hootenanny including Dominican Sisters who performed. College students and St. Joe's high school seniors attended. [209]

St. Joe's alumni in Lansing developed Teens Encounter Christ in 1965.

Internal activities

The last SCAS meeting was in September 1966. [211] In 1968 plans were made to start a yearbook. [212] 10 students from five area high schools came to the seminary for a day to promote inter-scholastic understanding and perhaps develop a city-wide student council. [213]

A student account of the 1960's

The items from *St. Joseph's Recorder* tell some of what happened during the 1960's but the real stories never made the paper. Fr. Dennis Morrow was a student at St. Joe's from 1962-1968 and he recalled several incidents that flesh out the changes that were taking place and make the story very human.

> *The 1965-66 year was tumultuous. I remember how we laughed when word got around the student body that a new freshman (I think in September, 1965) had mouthed off to a faculty member who corrected or contradicted him on something, "Don't you talk to me like that, or I'll tell my folks!!" All of us thought that hysterical, not because the jig was up for the seminary authority, but because our folks didn't have anything to do with what went on behind the "Burton curtain." We were as amazed and amused as the faculty would have been at the very suggestion that a stupid "firstie" would think his folks had any say about what happened at the Sem. We were in our own separate world, except for vacation time, when we pierced the bubble for a while and re-entered the earth's atmosphere.*
>
> *Yet this little incident conveys very well the change that was taking place in society and just barely touching the church at this point.*
>
> *I was in 4th year (senior high), living on the 3rd floor of St. Henry's with the two college years on the 1st and 2nd floors. We were heavily influenced by the college guys, who were rebelling against their religion prof, Msgr. Shaw. Almost every class was an argument, and at lunch the stories would abound about Shaw's retrenchment and the students (fueled by the NCR [National Catholic Reporter] and some of the younger clergy) wanting to see and experience more change that they thought the Council was envisioning and calling for. We had our own problems with OUR religion prof, Fr. Bissot. He was a very stubborn and forceful man back then, and would sometimes shout us down in class when he thought we were becoming theologically obnoxious (which we probably were, but it was "no holds barred"! He and I get along very well now when we see each other, I think he's still pastor up around West Branch). There were further arguments about what we*

48

considered to be too-restrictive discipline. This all resulted in a
"protest" march on March 7, 1966 (a free day, St. Thomas Aquinas back
then) on the front driveway under Bissot's window during compulsory
recreation. It was bitter, bitter cold that day, and some of the students
had come in early just to warm up. Bissot came down and threw them
out, so a bunch joined them and they all sang "We Shall Overcome"
under his window. He got mad and went over to Msgr. Moran and told
him to look out the window. Things escalated after that. Students
(primarily the senior house, or St. Henry's) and faculty got into a tug of
war over almost everything. Town meetings were held, demands were
made, and finally there was a meeting with Msgr. Moran in which the
students had the "senior deacon" of the 6th year class read an
ultimatum: Moran, Shaw, and Bissot had to go. Moran handled it very
well, actually, and very pointedly said that his responsibility was to the
Church and the Bishop. He would not be pressured into making
changes that he thought were unhealthy or ill-timed.

One of the significant changes that came about in the spring of
1966 was the organization of a Seminary Board of Counsel, [214] of which
my mother, Marian Morrow, was among the first members. The Board
was made up of several seminarian parents and several lay Catholics
selected by Msgr. Moran. They met for some time with Monsignor and
with faculty members to work out different approaches to discipline,
schedule changes, and the addressing of other concerns. In 1968-69 a
Public Relations Committee was formed as part of the Advisory Board.
[215]

But some changes began to be made, rather soon. Long-time
regulations were eased, there was a more relaxed atmosphere about
discipline (although the air was still often full of tension when Shaw and
Bissot were around). We did have a meeting with Bishop Babcock,
which was unspectacular. He listened, but basically dismissed our
concerns and later told the faculty that we were upset about "lumps in
the milk." At the end of the school year (June, 1966), Shaw and Bissot
were indeed transferred, along with Msgr. Martin (whom everyone
actually liked) and Fr. Ancona (who was something of a folk hero for all
of us). Ancona's removal was a great blow to all of us and to him.
Anyway, after all that, word of course got around the diocese, and the
polarization of clergy got pretty heated. The priests, who were
responsible for getting 8th grade students to Field Day for an
introduction to seminary life, began to be affected by the same malaise
and uncertainty and anger that was afflicting us. The enrollment began
to drop almost immediately. All this was really quite unforeseen, since
in 1965, architect's plans had been drawn up to build a new chapel wing

extending out onto the front lawn, and to build the other half of St. Henry's. What is there is basically half the building it was designed to be. The four classrooms, 66 student rooms, and 6 faculty suites were to be expanded to 8, 132, and 12 by building a mirror-image structure just to the east. Of course, all those plans were shelved when the precipitous decline in enrollment occurred. Saginaw had unfortunately in the early 1960's just completed its St. Paul's Seminary, which I don't think had much more than 10 really solid years of life.

Several parents had become alarmed around Christmas time when one of our classmates, Patrick O'Neill from St. Thomas parish in Grand Rapids, had developed pneumonia (as I recall). After a few days in the infirmary, Sister Christopher decided that his condition was not improving, and he was taken to St. Mary's Hospital, where he spent a couple of days. After his return to the Seminary his parents found out he had been admitted to the hospital and subsequently discharged, and they had never been informed. Word quickly spread among the parents, especially Grand Rapids parents, who had been hearing various things about the Seminary from their students and were beginning to talk among themselves--something that had never really happened before, but which made sense in the atmosphere of questioning and challenging that was becoming a new standard in both Church and society.

As I recall, Msgr. Sweeney, the pastor of St. Thomas, counseled O'Neill's parents to have nothing to do with any parent group, so they were not involved themselves. (That's indicative of the polarization of the clergy which was already on the rise, although Sweeney was a beloved long-time pastor who just wouldn't have wanted his people to make trouble.)

I know that Irene Swart from St. Stephen's, a sister of Fr. John Breitenstein, who had two sons at St. Joseph's, was an outspoken member. And as I recall, Albin Schinderle, an attorney from Big Rapids, whose son Ron was in the class ahead of us, also was involved.

The whole incident about O'Neill outraged some parents, but I remember that it seemed to be nothing unusual to us as students. The whole atmosphere of the seminary in those days was that we had left the world and its attachments, and the faculty was responsible for us. It never occurred to us that our parents would or should be involved in anything that happened or in any decisions that were made. We were like the classical "perfect society," self-contained and self-sufficient.

I am sure this was not unlike other religious schools, military schools, or Indian schools. Everyone trusted the authorities to do the right thing and take the necessary actions. And, by and large, they did!

Another contemporary commented on the O'Neill controversy this way, "It was like we had gone to a religious order and were of age. They assumed in loco parentis responsibility without even informing parents they were doing so. It was quite different by 1976. We had parental release forms, etc."

Msgr. Gaspar F. (Gus) Ancona, who was on the Seminary faculty from September, 1963, to June, 1966, adds these comments to what was happening at St. Joe's in the mid-1960's:

"One thing we may have underestimated at the time--and maybe still-- was the climate of change in our country and in Europe, even pedagogically, from authoritarian structures and styles to participative. Notably, too, in the liturgy. Another backdrop for us in this country, was the so-called free- speech movement at the Univ. of Calif. in Berkley. So, what began to happen within our previously closed seminary system was, in its own way, reflective of greater changes happening on a larger scale across society. Your evocation of the role parents played was, to me, particularly moving. Here were devoted and utterly sincere true-blue Catholics speaking frankly, respectfully, and for the first time boldly to church authorities about their concerns for their children. It was, and remains, an astonishment to all."

College Students go to Aquinas

In 1965-66 the college department began to separate from the high school. That year 33 College students took classes in physics and music appreciation at Aquinas College in Grand Rapids. [216] It was hoped that integration of seminarians with regular college students would be of benefit to all but for some reason all the music appreciation students were seminarians and only three of the physics students were not seminarians.

Starting in September 1966, the college students took all their classes at Aquinas but lived in St. Henry's They had morning and evening prayer in St. Henry's Hall and Mass in the late afternoon in the main chapel, separate from the high school. Father (later Bishop) Rose was the dean of the College Dept., and they would have one hour of class, either Latin or religion depending on the day of the week, at 8 a.m. before the yellow school bus picked them up at 9 and took them to Aquinas for all of the other classes. Then they got back on the bus at 3 and went back to Burton Street. This arrangement continuedfor two years through June, 1969.

The Diocese of Grand Rapids purchased the old Thomas (a local grocery magnate) mansion at 2001 Robinson Rd., S.E. as the college seminarians' residence and called it Christopher House. In September, 1969, it opened.

It was a grand old mansion with many rooms and an attic and a basement, but there were students EVERYWHERE! Fire regulations required enclosing the magnificent stairway, adding to the crowdedness. Within a year or two, an addition was built on the east end, which made things much more comfortable. Fr. Dennis Morrow thought the maximum in residence hit 32 at one point. Within a few years the enrollment was plummeting. By about 1990, it was too much building. The Diocese sold it to Aquinas College and moved the Christopher House operation to St. Stephen's Convent at 723 Rosewood Ave., S.E., in East Grand Rapids. Then that also eventually closed, on July 2, 2003.

This meant the Seminary campus had only high school students after 1969. This also meant that this was the end of the St. Joseph's Seminary as it had been established and operated for sixty years.

Enrollment and Graduation data

While the following enrollment chart is not complete, it helps us to make some interesting observations. Clearly the seminary building near the cathedral in 1913 was inadequate for the number of students wanting to be priests. The main building at 600 Burton Street was designed for 100 students. Already in the second year, there were over 100.

The Great Depression of the 1930's seriously affected enrollment. Fr. John Thome recalled that he was one of only 11 in his first year class in 1935. Total enrollment dropped by a third by 1938-39 but then began an astonishing growth that did not reverse itself until the late 1950's. The decline then was just as dramatic.

It is worthwhile noting that the Diocese of Grand Rapids was the only diocese outside Detroit in the lower peninsula of Michigan until the 1930's. In 1937 the Diocese of Lansing was created and the Diocese of Saginaw in 1938. As a result enrollment was broken down by diocese after that. In the fall of 1943, 68 students were from the Diocese of Grand Rapids, 31 from Saginaw and 28 from Lansing. [217] The enrollment prior to the creation of the new dioceses most likely included students from the Lansing and Saginaw areas but those areas were in the Grand Rapids diocese. The Dioceses of Kalamazoo and Gaylord were established in 1971.

In 1945 the number of students from the Grand Rapids Diocese jumped to 93, Saginaw students increased to 33 and Lansing to 23. [218]

In 1956 St. Joseph's Seminary started the practice of requiring an entrance exam. A record number of 135 took the exam in the spring of 1963,[219] indicating a strong interest in the seminary.

The chart shows enrollment in September, by class, and an ending enrollment total in June. The number of sixth year students is the number who graduated. These figures are taken from the annual seminary *Bulletin* unless otherwise noted.

Students left during the school year either by choice or involuntarily resulting in a gradual decrease over the year. I think this was a phenomenon that developed as the enrollment shot up. The year 1952-53 is the only school year where I found beginning and ending numbers for each class. In that year 25 left the seminary during the year but only 20 left in the 1955-56 year even though there were more enrolled. .

There was a record enrollment in 1956-57 at 237 but 44 students left during that year. The following year held the record for enrollment at 240 but 53 students left before the end of the year. Enrollment held fairly strong until 1965-66 when the total number in the seminary at the end of the year was down to 121.

By 1968-69 the total number of students dropped below 100 for the first time since the late 1930's. Beginning in 1969-70 the total number of students includes the college students who were living at Christopher House near Aquinas College and taking classes there, not at the seminary. This meant that only 67 high school students were at the seminary. There were only 49 the following year, then 40, when they moved into St. Henry's.

Year	Sept	1st	2nd	3rd	4th	5th	6th	June
1921-22							7 [220]	
1922-23	100+ [221]							
1923-24	92 [222]							
1924-25	94 [223]	28	10	15	20	9	12	95
1925-26	93 [224]	25	19	10	11	20	8 [225]	95
1926-27		22	12	10	10	10	15 [226]	102
1927-28	105	33	26	17	13	6	8	104
1928-29		25	27	20	14	11	7	104
1929-30							10 [227]	
1930-31	111 [228]	20	25	17	18	16	14	112
1931-32	118 [229]						14 [230]	
1938-39	67 [231]						5 [232]	
1939-40	76 [233]						9 [234]	
1940-41	76 [235]						10 [236]	
1941-42							10 [237]	
1942-43	109 [238]						11 [239]	
1943-44	130 [240]						11 [241]	
1944-45	158 [242]						13 Feb [243]	
1945-46	145 [244]						7 Oct. [245]	
1946-47	186 [246]						15 [247]	
1947-48							19 [248]	
1949-50							16 [249]	

1950-51		74 [250]					11 [251]	
1951-52							19 [252]	
1952-53 [253]	175	59	38	26	27	13	10	
End of year		49	36	25	19	12	9	150
1953-54		39	31	24	23	14	10	146 [254]
1954-55		41	25	25	21	19	17	148
1955-56	209 [255]	63	29	24	23	19	19	189 [256]
1956-57	236 [257]	54	48	23	27	20	20	192
1957-58	240 [258]	57	32	38	17	25	18	187
1958-59		54	47	25	30	15	25	196
1959-60		35	37	13	13	25	14	139 [259]
1960-61		64	24	26	23	10	21	168
1961-62		54	35	13	21	20	10	153
1962-63		54	44	30	26	5	17	176
1963-64		52	34	32	16	23	3	160
1964-65		50	26	24	23	11	19	153
1965-66		37	32	16	17	16	3	121
1966-67		27	27	22	11	15	11	113
1967-68		14	22	22	18	14	13	103
1968-69		19	13	19	18	13	11	93
1969-70		23	17	10	17	10	11	88
1970-71		13	10	16	10	13	9	71
1971-72		12	6	11	11	7	9	56

Graduation

I must emphasize that the focus of the seminary was solely on training for the priesthood and so the seminary did not consider the implications for a student who finished high school at St. Joseph's but chose not to continue studies for the priesthood. In 1958-1959 my class was the first to actually receive a high school diploma. St. Joseph's Seminary had affiliated with Catholic University and that University gave us a high school diploma. Unfortunately my diploma had Norman Bufka instead of Norbert Bufka so it was not very special to me and, fortunately, I never needed to show the actual diploma.

The real graduation from St. Joe's was the completion of the six years of study. "From 1914 to 1919 the Juniors used to give a banquet for the graduating Seniors. Formal graduation exercises that we [had in 1961] began in 1921." [260] Graduation day was marked with celebration of Mass and granting of diplomas. They were, of course, written in Latin. Families came to celebrate with us and of course take us home with all of our earthly possessions.

The big excitement of the day was the letter of appointment we received from the Rector Fr. James P. Moran. I quickly opened my letter to read:

June 7, 1961

Dear Mr. Bufka:

I wish to inform you that the Most Reverend Bishop has assigned you to Mt. St. Mary's Seminary, Norwood Ohio.

May God bless your work and strengthen your desire for the Holy Priesthood.

Sincerely in Christ,
(Signed)

I was disappointed. I had been hoping for an appointment to St. Mary's Seminary and University in Baltimore. But I got over my disappointment and left St. Joseph's with my family. I believe I spent the summer working with the migrants in Leelanau County.

Impact of seminary on life after leaving

It is hard to evaluate the success of St. Joseph's Seminary but we can make a few significant comments. From a report written in 1960, there were approximately 500 ordinations of students who attended the seminary from three dioceses. Nine of them were ordained bishops: Edmund C. Szoka, Robert J. Rose, Joseph C. McKinney, Paul V. Donovan, Joseph Green, Kenneth J. Povish, James A. Hickey Charles A. Salatka, and James S. Sullivan. James A. Hickey and Edmund C. Szoka became Cardinals. [261]

Norbert 1961-62

After graduating from St. Joe's, I had to prepare for the major seminary. The mandatory attire was cassock and collar. I needed two cassocks, one for every day and one for dress up. (That's me in the picture in 1961-62).

Since Norwood is a city within Cincinnati it was too far away for my parents or family to drive me there and I looked for alternative ways to travel. I found an overnight train from Kalkaska, Michigan to Cincinnati. To save money I sat in the coach section rather than a sleeper. During the trip the Pennsylvania Railroad, owners of that train, gave passengers a set of six souvenir glasses because it was the last time they were making that run.

In recent years I learned that my classmate, Jim Beckstrom, was also on that train but I do not remember him being on it nor did he remember me being there. We both found that very odd since we lived near each other. Jim lived in Traverse City and I lived on a farm about twenty miles northwest of Traverse City. Jim's luggage did not arrive with him and he spent the first few days at the seminary awaiting his luggage.

After being at Mt. St. Mary's just a few short weeks I had very serious doubts about continuing. I felt very different about being a priest than I had for five years at St. Joe's. After the fall seven day silent retreat I decided to continue but the doubts remained. During the seven day silent retreat in the spring I decided to leave.

When I told my friends that I was not returning in the fall of 1962, Ron Schneider exclaimed, "Norb, you are the last person I would have thought to leave the seminary." That shocked me but I did not change my mind.

Shortly after arriving home, Mom said to me, "You act like a big load has been lifted from your shoulders." I knew I had made the right decision. I had been in the seminary out of obligation more than desire. Suddenly I had some decisions to make about my future. I thought seriously of going into the Air Force, like my brother Ray had done, but Mom suggested I finish my bachelor's degree since I had only one more year to complete. I knew some of my former classmates were attending Aquinas College in Grand Rapids and so I applied there and was accepted.

I loved history so I majored in that subject. Aquinas required 45 semester hours in residence to earn a degree there and I had six hours left after fulfilling my major requirements. I took two courses in education and decided to be a teacher. I went back to Aquinas and earned my teaching certificate in the fall of 1963. I did my student teaching at Grand Rapids Catholic Central High School in Latin. I was teaching on that fateful day of November 22, 1963 when President Kennedy was assassinated.

In January 1964 I wasn't sure about my future and thought again about entering the Air Force. Instead however I accepted a teaching position at the same school where I did my student teaching. My assignments were American Literature and American History. I was the third teacher for these students that year. It was a baptism of fire into teaching.

Yet I had many doubts now about my future. The very harsh warning of Msgr. Falicki that I would always be known as an ex-seminarian and therefore a failure dogged me for a long time. Fortunately for me, my class had a number of reunions which I was able to attend. I learned I was not alone in my anxiety.

I blamed the seminary life for a lot of what was wrong in my life for many years. It wasn't until I was in therapy in the 1990's that I learned of my own serious emotional and psychological immaturity that was much of the cause of my anxieties.

Life at the seminary had its rewards and benefits however. I have never abandoned prayer or my Catholic Church although it has been very tempting of late. Seminary life instilled in me a very studious behavior which has helped not only in my college years but throughout life. I still love to study, do research, and of late write books, like this one.

Seminary life had also made me many friends for whom I am grateful. I can talk to them about seminary life and my life and they understand.

I always said the discipline was oppressive and that it did not teach me to have self-discipline. I still think that is true but a classmate told me that he thought it was the best thing for him.

On a very practical level, it gave me the path to a college education which might have been impossible otherwise. It definitely started me on an academic path.

Other students of St. Joseph's Seminary shared some thoughts with me about how their lives at St. Joe's were impacted after leaving the seminary. The following reflections are in their own words.

Jim Beckstrom

1955-1961, Class of 1961

Beginning with Msgr. Martin's logic course (not that we hadn't been focusing on the "logical" side of life the whole time), and continuing with the heavy hitter courses at Norwood for senior college, St. Joe's provided an immersion in the mind set of what it took to do computer systems analysis. Secondarily, all of the foreign language studies provided lots of practice translating, a very essential skill for converting company departmental needs into computer software-eze.

I have been athletically active all my life - played a lot of handball the 3 following years in school, lots of racquet ball for some years afterwards, and various and sundry sports ever since.

George Fulk, 1955-61

George was a member of my Class of 1961 but left before graduation. In a letter to our classmate, Bob Lesinski, in 1973, he recalled these random memories of life at St. Joe's:

Watching "You are there" with Walter Cronkite' on Sunday night, listening to [Msgr. Joseph]Shaw read Homer [in Greek], singing the Holy Week liturgy in the choir, kneeling for 3 hours straight during 'tre ore', smelling incense during benediction, singing 'Urbs' from the Liber Usualis, figuring out what Usualis meant, ice skating on the pond, digging tree stumps out for St. Henry's, taking a 3-minute shower after tennis with Frank Fallon, watching the firemen dust off the statue of St. Joseph, grand silence in the big first year dormitory, eating hot whole wheat bread, weeping during my last Sunday mass at St. Joe's.

[By way of explanation, "tre ore" was the three hours on Good Friday commemorating Jesus' hanging on the cross. Urbs was the first word of a chant that George loved. There apparently was a fire drill in which the fire department came to test their ladder's extension to the fourth floor. While at the top of the ladder, the fireman dusted off the statue of St. Joseph.]

In October 2014 George shared these thoughts with me regarding life at St. Joe's and its impact on him:

Normally the human brain cleans up memories and makes them nice, much more pleasant than the actual fact. For me that is not the case with my seminary days. I do have pleasant memories of the friendships and good times on the sports field and in the summer and with the choir. However, my brain has not been able to put a happy face on the discipline, the emphasis on memorization to the detriment of creativity and critical thinking. Moran and Falicki stir up only negative feelings. I guess they meant well, but I think were gravely mistaken about how to motivate boys/young men to enter the religious life. We were just too young to be making those important decisions when we entered the seminary at age 14. What stupidity!

"Leaving St. Joe's was very traumatic for me. I knew I could not hold up the celibacy requirement. I wanted to have a close sexual relationship with a woman and I wanted a family. Still I wanted to be a priest. It was a hard choice. I hated leaving my friends. I hated "quitting" what I had worked hard for. I remember breaking grand silence for many hours the night I left, talking to Myron Hawkins who actually came into my room at St. Henry's so we could talk. That was the first and last time I had anyone in my room there. I was afraid because I knew "readjustment to the real world" would be difficult and I had no idea what to do with my life.

Fr. Den Morrow

Attended six years 1962-1968 and graduated,

As the years go on, I grow ever more grateful to the people of the Diocese for their generosity in providing the seminary education I had at St. Joseph's. I am astounded at the breadth and depth of knowledge we acquired there, which quickly built on my native inquisitiveness, as well as on my love for language and history. The rich religious formation I had received in the family and in the Catholic grade school was further developed by the opportunities offered behind "the Burton Curtain." To this day I fondly remember so many elements of liturgy and devotion which we learned and which I have incorporated into my own spiritual life. I had the privilege of beginning high school a month before the Second Vatican Council began, and I can vividly remember Monsignor Shaw leading the rosary each Friday evening for the intention of "the success of the Council." (At that point, he was still very excited about it. His prayers were answered, but not always in the ways he might have expected!) Under the capable direction of the faculty, we learned about the theology behind liturgical reform, ecumenism, respect for non-Christians, and the call of discipleship to plunge deeply into the world and its joys and sorrows.

There were negatives, true. But even those taught us how to bear up under hardship, to persevere, to survive bureaucracy, and to endeavor to get along in close quarters with those who were disagreeable. What lessons for diocesan and parish life! And how we learned that sometimes WE were the ones being disagreeable! We engaged in parliamentary procedure at SCAS meetings. We asked silly questions about world affairs like the perpetual "What can we as seminarians do?" (as though anyone else cared). We engaged in the adolescent dreams of saving the world once we emerged from our cocoon. In spite of our segregation from the rest of society and from the opposite sex, we for the most part resiliently bounded into adulthood with a solid work ethic, an appreciation for the benefits of leisure and recreation, more than an ounce of compassion for those in need, and a capacity to form deep and lasting relationships. And most of us can answer Jeopardy! questions better than anyone else in the room. Now, if you disagree and don't share my opinions, can I at least have your dessert?

Edward Hahnenberg
Attended 1955-1961, graduated 1961

St Joseph's Seminary was the environment God chose for me....the best teachers and education I could have received. After 1961 I spent 2 years at St. Mary's Seminary and University on Paca St. in Baltimore. There I met Fr. Eugene Walsh who had a great influence on my life. It was also the town where scripture scholar Fr. Raymond Brown taught...the most respected biblical scholar whose writings I hold immensely important in my faith life. They helped in my 2nd MA...with scripture as a major.

James Dalrymple
1955-57, Class of 1961

I was only there a year or so. I left and went into the Franciscans. Both places had a profound impact.

Saint Joe's taught me discipline and perseverance and the knowledge that if I can make it at Saint Joe's I can make it anywhere. It instilled a sense of confidence, but I didn't realize it until many years later.

The Latin and Greek gave me the basis to ace the foreign language test when I was dragged into the military. That got me into language school to learn Russian. They sent me to Japan where I learned Japanese, then German and on and on. I even got my first job in a Chicago bank "because if you can speak Russian I can teach you anything." or so they thought. It all started at Saint Joe's. And I'm still not in therapy yet. "Get ready." says my wife, Judy.

But what really stands out in my mind is the army basic training where we were harshly treated and under severe discipline. One terrified guy looked at me and asked: "Why you always smilin'? You like it here?" "Hey - compared to Saint Joe's - this is a piece of cake. They feed you, they pay you, they clothe you and even give you 30 days paid vacation." And so it was.

John Mullally

1956-61, Class of 1961

As a 1961 graduate of St. Joseph Seminary College, I have thought and often discussed the impact of these years on my developing teenage person. During these critical teenage years to trade a loving home life for an impersonal institutional life had the potential for a catastrophic psychological train-wreck. As I celebrate my 50th wedding anniversary this year [2015] I can honestly say I persevered and prospered through my life with the help of my St. Joe years.

Academically, I received an exclusive prep school education that instilled the necessity of hard work (study!) to achieve success. The mandatory recreation periods reinforced the" mens sana in corpore sana" mantra in my daily life. The ring of the ten-minute bell while we were still out on the ball fields taught me alacrity: to shower, dress and get to the study hall before the final bell rang. The prayers and religious devotions were a given in the semjnary setting. However, the 6:30 AM morning meditation often was a time to catch additional shut-eye without falling out of the pew!

This minor seminary's pre-Vatican II Council closed lifestyle seems like ancient history. Even though it appeared to work for a number of years, the evolving changes in the church, secular society and family life preclude it ever returning. Amen to an important period of personal as well as church history.

Fr. Paul Milanowski

1953-1959, Class of 1959, ordained 1965.

In retrospect, I can say I really appreciate my seminary experience (major seminary more than minor).

I've told many that, but also said I would never encourage anyone to enter a minor seminary today.

Boys and girls boarding schools and military academies were an accepted part of the times back then.

But, at the time, I'm not so sure I was all that thrilled about a number of aspects of minor seminary life.

It was a "hothouse" experience, and definitely not a normal experience of teenage development in ordinary family life.

In my eighth grade at St Andrew's Cathedral, before entering the seminary, I was captivated by the daily schedule and routine as found in the small green Rule Book. I think I needed some kind of strict schedule for my life. I needed the discipline of study halls to get my work done. I was not a good student. I procrastinated. I was not good at deadlines and assignments.

I was very poor in math; in fact I failed both John Bellardo's classes of algebra and geometry. (But he taught with my Dad at Aquinas, and passed me anyway, saying: " Mr. Milanowski, you probably won't ever use math if you're a priest!")

Like Fr. William Shannon, *Seeking The Face of God,* p. 5, and many other seminary products of my era, we 'said' lots of prayers every day, year after year, but I don't think I was ever taught to pray. We, (students and faculty and spiritual director) took it for granted. At least that was my experience.

The Rector and Faculty were a major factor in our lives. I recall only one teacher who ever really inspired me in the subject he was teaching. That was Fr. Noel P. Fay. Several were very kind and considerate. The rest were either insignificant or harmful. Early in life I decided I would not act or behave like them. It was mostly an adversarial situation between faculty and students. I learned quickly to stay under the radar -and avoided any marks in conduct throughout high school. I was always attracted to music and finally being selected to be in the seminary choir, under the direction of a caring and gifted faculty member, Fr. John J. Thome, I somehow survived and thrived those days of opposition between 'them' and 'us'.

Good grades and good in athletics, and the students with one or both, were highly favored in the system. The classmates who took advantage of this were called 'suckies' or 'brown noses'. I was at the very bottom of this list as I excelled in neither. As a result I was never chosen to be a 'prefect' or hold any one of the many student jobs in the academic, athletic, or cultural structure of the seminary. The only job I had was my senior year as stage manager -probably the very lowest on the pecking order and list of favoritism.

The most beneficial part of minor seminary was a close fraternal life with others my age. Close and personal friendships were strictly forbidden, but friendship and camaraderie were a vital and sustaining part of everyday life. Though friendships with upperclassmen were forbidden too, they were a kind of inspiration and support to the lower classmen. High motivation and exceptional personal qualities were in abundance among the students. When some left and decided not to continue, or others were dismissed, expelled or asked to leave, it was a heart-wrenching experience, especially if they were good friends. Another strict rule was that we were never to write or associate with anyone who left the seminary. (I always found that intolerable and in opposition to the heart of the Gospel!)

Unfortunately I missed out on six years of ordinary family life with my mother and father, my older brother and sister, and three younger brothers, my two grandmothers, and a very big Polish family -on my father's side.

Although I was befriended and inspired by several parish priests (assistants at the Cathedral) I was never shown any consideration by my pastor.

Chuck Neubecker

September 1955 to June 1958, Class of 1961.

St. Joe's affected my life in four ways: community life/discipline, education, physical well-being, and spirituality.

The community life at St. Joseph's taught me to get along with others, be attentive to others' needs, and to assist others. It also taught me to organize myself and to be on time. Others have commented at our reunions how being reminded by a bell helped them organize themselves. This also was good preparation for the Army, which in many cases is more demanding than living in one large building. My time in Korea on the border with North Korea was time-consuming and stressful, often working on many projects simultaneously over considerable distances. But at the same time Korean service was fulfilling. You either organize yourself and those dependent upon you or you fail in your mission.

Education at St. Joe's was fantastic – classical education that few receive outside such an institution. We had excellent instructors and they taught us how to think. Foreign languages are also very good for the brain. I was a witness to the explosion in the Chemistry lab at St. Joe's and remember being taken to the ER at the Hospital for a slight wound in the belly. Maybe that accident catalyzed my interest in Chemistry? My first year at Michigan State in engineering was difficult since I had to make the transition from classical education to something technical and mathematical. My favorite anecdote there was when the calculus teacher asked me my major after it was apparent that I had no clue what calculus was all about. I proudly responded "Chemical engineering". She replied, "You better think about changing your major." Luckily I figured it out in time.

I was never much of an athlete at St. Joe's and not much afterwards either. But I figured out that one does not need to be an athlete to become physically fit. In the Army I struggled to pass the fitness test for the Army Airborne School but with a lot of individual practice, did so. Three weeks at hot and humid Fort Benning, Georgia in June 1965 were the more physically strenuous time in my life, but by the grace of God I survived and got my airborne wings with five jumps. I've tried to stay fit since then and have done several walking half marathons. Still not much of an athlete though.

I don't think I would have had the fortitude to do this had it not been for the athletic regimen at St. Joe's.

All of the above means nothing if our relationship with God is nonexistent or lacking. St. Joe's taught me much about faith, the Bible, the magisterium, and the necessity of good works, which should accompany faith. After leaving the seminary I have tried first of all to live my faith in my job, my family life, and my extracurricular life. In the Army in Korea I got involved in helping orphanages and decades later did similar things in Ukraine. After the tragic Roe versus Wade decision in 1973 I got involved in pro-life activities to the extent that time permitted and the opportunities presented themselves. Since 1999 I've had a lot more time to spend on pro-life work. I've also tried to instill in my children and grandchildren Catholic faith and values. One final anecdote – I made two business trips to Communist Vietnam in the early 1970's. The Church was very much persecuted then, but due to the strong faith of Vietnamese Catholics, the government was forced to keep the churches open (like in Poland). At Mass at Notre Dame Cathedral in Saigon I attended the most fervent Mass of my life, despite the not so secret police keeping an eye on me. Whenever I checked out of a hotel, I just happened to forget and leave some Catholic literature in the room, knowing that their thirst for literature in English would cause them not to throw it away.

My life at St. Joseph's Seminary was a wonderful experience that has helped me throughout life.

Dennis Wasco

Attended 1955-1961, Class of 1961, Ordained 1967, left priestly ministry 1971.

I have mixed emotions about the time that I spent at St. Joseph Seminary in Grand Rapids. I was there before the Vatican Council and the seminary at that time was the product and victim of a medieval Church and unenlightened psychology. I would like to highlight the positives that I experienced

In the seminary I developed some lasting friendships with wonderful human beings, who have gone on to accomplish great things in their lives and with their families. It was almost in spite of the seminary experience that we were successful. We built lasting bonds having endured situations that few others will ever understand or appreciate. That is why I feel so close to my "brothers" and why they are more than just "classmates". Although some were scarred by the experience, most of us are able to laugh about those difficult days and reminisce on what we endured. These are lifelong friends, whose friendship and companionship I treasure.

Although a curriculum heavy in Latin and Greek hardly prepared me for a career in business, I learned the skills of goal setting and time management, which were definite helps in later life. I developed a love for history and reading during those years. An interest in politics and social justice came from discussions with my classmates. Although our spiritual life was more directed to monastic life, it laid the groundwork for a growth in faith and a Scriptural-centered spirituality.

In hindsight the Church could have provided a better learning experience for its future leaders, but it was a victim of its own short-sightedness and past history.

John Schultz

Attended 1954-60, ordained 1966, left priestly ministry 1973.

As a "lifer", I entered the seminary after 8th grade in September, 1954, graduating (Falicki would say "moving on") from there in June, 1960. Like many who attended the seminary in Grand Rapids, the memories are myriad.

One of the profs referred to St. Joe's one day as the "West Point of the Midwest." How accurate that epithet was in wider seminary circles, I'll never know. I *do* know, however, that St. Joe's very well equipped us for any curriculum or regimen that *any* major seminary in the East or Midwest had to offer.

I have often said that we survived *in spite of* the rigid system there. In the same breath I have also noted what an excellent curriculum we experienced there. The education in classical languages alone (Latin and Greek) was outstanding, to say nothing of the English & Speech curriculum (which included literature, of course) plus Ancient, American and European history. What a well-rounded Humanities program!

The seminary curriculum in philosophy at Catholic University in Washington, D.C., included a number of textbooks in Latin. No problem! After C.U., I was sent to the North American College in Rome to study theology at the Gregorian. The very first day Prof. Rene Latourelle from Montreal launched into his introductory lecture on Revelation *in Latin*, followed by an American, a Spaniard and an Italian all doing the same. Again, no problem. Thanks to 6 years of Latin at St. Joe's, I just listened and wrote the notes in English. Some years later I would end up teaching Latin myself in two different high schools and loved every minute.

J.P Moran inspired in me an everlasting love of history. (I'm sure I have lots of company here.) As a result, I have taught church history seminars and classes with a personal passion for 40 some years to students ranging from teens to older adults. Thanks, J.P.!

One of my high school students used to write down and try to learn new words that she would encounter. She told me one day that she learned more of these in my world religions class than anywhere else. Thanks, St. Joe's Humanities curriculum!

We had some excellent teachers among the profs at St. Joe's. I never forgot them and tried to emulate the best ones when I was a seminary prof myself at St. Paul Seminary, Saginaw, from 1967 to 1971. In a word, I took a lot of St. Joe's with me when I left there in June of 1960. *Ad multos annos*!

I took a leave of absence from priestly ministry in 1973 and was laicized and married in August, 1977.

Fr. John J. Thome

Attended 1935-1941, Ordained 1946, professor 1946-1965.

St. Joe's seminary prepared students to face and challenge a world of relativism.   For many people, "do it your way".   "Do what makes you feel good."   "Anything you choose is the right way for you".   "You are the Judge".   A good classical education prepares one to be accurate in thinking and choosing.   You cannot put any ending on words like nouns and verbs. Latin and Greek have declensions and conjugations. If you put a nominative ending where it should be accusative or dative, you got red lines under the mistakes and a poor mark.   You can never say that anything goes, it does not matter what ending you put on the words. .   Students from St. Joe's found college courses less difficult than students from most high-schools. And the discipline helped to keep us from thinking that we could do it better "my way".   Not all the professors were overly rigorous disciplinarians. Like many teachers they did their best for the benefit of all the students, even though some students do not realize it at the time.

3 History and Campus

Cathedral, Grand Rapids, Mich.

June 22, 1909

Rev. dear Father:-

We intend to open a Preparatory Seminary in the City of Grand Rapids in the beginning of next September. The students who have already, with Our permission, entered a Seminary will continue their studies therein, but all those who have not as yet been in a Seminary must enter the one which We are about to open in Grand Rapids. "The Holy Synod ordains," says the Council of Trent, "that all Cathedral Churches...shall be bound, each according to its means and the extent of the diocese, to maintain, to educate religiously, and to train in ecclesiastical discipline, a certain number of youth of their city or diocese, in a college to be chosen by the Bishop for this purpose near the said churches."

You will, please, at your earliest convenience, and not later than the 15th of July next, inform Us if you have any candidates for the Seminary in your parish, so that proper preparation for their reception may be made. All candidates must have finished, at least, the seventh grade of the Grammar School.

I remain, Dear Father,

Yours sincerely in Xto

HENRY JOSEPH
Bishop of Grand Rapids

Letter announcing the seminary startup

The first bishop of the Diocese of Grand Rapids, Henry Joseph Richter, had a fond wish to start a seminary but funds were limited in this new diocese created in 1883. In 1905 or so Pope Pius X encouraged him to proceed with developing a seminary.

In 1906 Bishop Richter brought in Monsignor Anthony Volkert, a native of Munster, Germany, and at that time the rector of the diocesan seminary at Nepi-Sutri Italy, to help develop the seminary.

In 1909 Bishop Richter purchased a frame building just south of St. Andrew's Cathedral on Sheldon Avenue as the first seminary building. On September 8, he dedicated the seminary to St. Joseph and appointed Volkert as the first rector. Volkert served the seminary until 1919 when he resigned because of ill health. Apparently he recovered as he retired after 33 years of service in 1942. [262] Volkert taught Greek and Latin. Other professors were: Rev. Salvatore Cianci, professor of Italian; Rev. Michael J. Gallagher (later Bishop of Detroit) professor of Greek; and Rev. Andrew Narloch, professor of Latin. Students took some of their classes at Catholic Central High School. In 1910, a four story brick structure was ready for use by the Seminary which was later used by Catholic Central HS. In 1913 an addition was made to this four story structure but it, too, was too small to meet the increasing enrollment. Both the first frame building and the four story structure were removed, along with the old Bishop's house/rectory/chancery, about 1997-2000.

Ray Hoey was in the seminary on Sheldon Ave. in the 1910's. Ray told Fr. Dennis Morrow that it was not uncommon for Bishop Richter to come outdoors and walk over to the fence and talk to the seminarians when they were out for recreation.

Bishop Richter dreamed of a larger seminary and at his death in 1916 left a considerable sum of money for the construction of a new building. The new bishop, Edward D. Kelly, turned his attention in 1919 to the securing of a favorable site for a new seminary building. In June that year the Diocese purchased twenty-two acres [1] at 600 Burton St. SE. M-37 was routed on Burton St. at that time. The area was still rural with a large horse farm and riding stables to the south. In 1922 "the land west of the seminary was cleared of trees, staked into lots and two cement sidewalks constructed. The calf is gone", reported the student newspaper. [263]

When the property was sold in2008 there were only about seventeen acres. Fr. Dennis Morrow, archivist for the Diocese of Grand Rapids, figures that the seminary gave up four to five acres when Union Blvd. on the west, Martin Ave. on the east, and Winchell St. on the south were laid out later in the 1920's.

The cornerstone was laid on November 20, 1919. Students moved in during Christmas week of

Document in cornerstone

---

[1] The 1925-26 Bulletin said it was 20 acres.

1920. On January 19, 1921,[2] the building was solemnly blessed by Bishop Kelly in the presence of the clergy of the Grand Rapids and neighboring dioceses.

At the outset it was intended that St. Joseph's Seminary train the student as far as the course of philosophy in third and fourth year college. The program of studies consisted of a classical course of six years, four years of high school and two years of college. Lack of adequate space did not allow for the enrollment of all the students as boarders; hence during the period of occupancy of the building on Sheldon Avenue up to the year 1921, students residing in the city of Grand Rapids were enrolled as day scholars for the first five years of their studies, and as boarders the last year. All other students were enrolled as boarders. When it was' opened in 1909, there was an enrollment of thirty-two students, fourteen boarders and eighteen day students. When the new building on Burton Street was completed, all students without exception were required to enroll as boarders.

Campus on Burton Street

In 1940 "Tree planting work started on south boundary of grounds" [264] so in the 1950's the *Bulletin* could say that the grounds were hedged by a variety of beautiful trees. Among them were great oaks, surviving witnesses of the pioneer days of Western Michigan.

Standing back on an elevation 300 feet from Burton Street, the main building is approached by a broad semi-circular concrete drive. The enclosed portion and the grounds on either side of the drive comprise a grassy plot well-watered and set with trees and shrubs. At the rear of the building are handball alleys and a service entrance to the campus.

In the spring of 1952 a combination football field and baseball diamond was under construction. [265] Tennis courts were added. These must have been new fields and courts because all these facilities existed in 1925-26.[266] Geological conditions provided the best possible drainage, a feature that insured a maximum of usage for the campus in early spring and late fall. A rink, flooded in the winter, provided good skating.

In the spring of 1961 [267] a cyclone fence was erected around the east, south, and west sides of the campus "to keep neighbor kids from playing on the campus". However the three strands of barbed wire at the top of the fence leaned inward, suggesting the fence was erected to keep us inside!

---

[2] The original date for the dedication was January 12, but Msgr. Thomas D. Flannery of Alpena died on January 4. Bishop Kelly and many of the priests of the Diocese traveled to his funeral, which took place in Alpena on Tuesday, January 11. so the dedication was transferred to the 19th.

The Main Building

Main Building (view from northwest)

    The main building is E-shaped with a frontage of 152 feet, and faces the north. It is of red pressed-brick and Sandusky stone, fire-proof construction. The floors are, for the most part, terrazzo. Considerable care was taken in planning the main building and in making it one of the most suitable structures in the country in providing for the needs of young aspirants to the priesthood. Though luxury and superfluity have been avoided, nothing has been overlooked that contributes to the seminarian's proper development.

    In the summer of 1929 a new steam heating system was installed. It had "two steel riveted boilers with automatic stokers."[268]

    In the ten-foot high basement, which extends well above the ground, were located the kitchen and refectory (dining room), store, locker room, and recreation room. In the west wing, where the excavation extends deeper, was located a gymnasium. This space served also as an auditorium, and had in the north end, a fully equipped stage. All conveniences for presenting literary programs, dramas, and educational films, were provided.

    Fr. John J. Thome, who graduated from St. Joseph's Seminary in 1941, recalled that in the room between the kitchen and gym, below the chapel, were two bowling alleys. They were there in 1924 [269] but were removed in 1944 to make way for an enlarged recreation room. It was dubbed "the Den" and in later years had a TV.[270] It was also used as a classroom during the years of high enrollment and before St. Henry's Hall was finished. The tunnel from St. Henry's Hall emerges here.

Gym in Main Building in 1925

Gym set up for Presentation

Bowling Lanes 1925

Refectory 1925

Two sisters working in the kitchen

In 1928 a new refrigerator was installed in the kitchen. [271] The kitchen was modernized in1947 with three-shelf carts, new dish racks for the dishwasher, stainless steel sinks, fluorescent lighting and gas water heater rather than coal. [272]

On the first floor directly opposite the main entrance and occupying the central portion of the E, was the chapel. It had Romanesque architecture with furnishings harmonizing and well calculated to inspire devotion. The beautiful altars were of rigalico and Vermont marble; the finish was old ivory and gold. The rich windows of Munich stained glass portrayed those scenes from the Lord's life that more especially relate to the training of the priest.

The windows in the seminary chapel were very similar to the windows in the original chapel at Marywood, the motherhouse of the Dominican Sisters of Grand Rapids, and in Holy Rosary Church at Cedar, Michigan (Isadore). The Marywood windows were constructed in the early 1920's by the Emil Frey Art Glass Company of Germany and St. Louis.

In the spring of 1925, preliminary work was done for the installation of a new electric pipe organ in the chapel, which was done in the summer. [273] In 1962, new organ pipes were installed. [274]

In the fall of 1945, Bishop Haas donated new Stations of the Cross in the chapel. [275]

In keeping with some liturgical renewal that was occurring in the worldwide church in 1951, chapel renovation began. The communion rail was removed and two angels were lost as a result. As new lighting was being installed, the gym became the temporary chapel. [276]

In keeping with the expected continued increase in enrollment in 1965, architect's plans had been drawn up to build a new chapel wing extending out onto the front lawn but declining enrollment sent those plans to the scrap heap.[277]

Chapel 1925

Chapel in the 1950's

Chapel windows 1925

Study Hall 1925

The study hall and library occupied the west wing of the first floor in 1925-26 but as enrollment increased, the library was moved to the second floor. In those early days the sisters lived on the first floor where the infirmary was later. The faculty room of the 1950's was most likely used by the sisters as well since the faculty room, and priests' library were originally on the second floor which later became the student library.

In 1928 a priests' library was established [278] and in 1929 the late Fr. Maus of Saginaw donated 700 books to that library.[279]

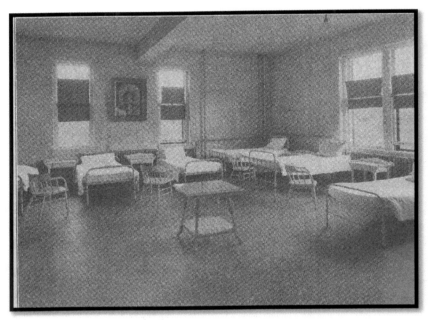

Infirmary on second floor 1925

On the second floor were the infirmary, the students' library, the professors' living quarters, recitation rooms and a laboratory with facilities for experiments in chemistry and biology.

In 1925 "A new fluoroscope, euscope and very high-powered microscope have been added to the lab." [280] In 1955 there was a renovation in the science classroom with installation of seven new lab tables. [281]

In 1922 the student library contained six thousand volumes. [282] In June 1926, the library received a bequest of nearly 1,000 books from the late Bishop Kelly. [283] in 1954 the library was expanded, taking the place of a linen closet, with an entrance into the adjoining room 207.[284] Fr. Weisengoff donated several books to the library including many by Zane Grey.

76

In the fall of 1962, a language lab was installed in rooms 207 and 208.

Classroom in Main Building 1925

The third floor was occupied principally by dormitories, bathrooms, showers, and locker rooms.

All parts of the building, especially the study hall and classrooms, were well provided with natural and artificial light. The blower type system of ventilation, spacious corridors, and high ceilings provided excellent circulation of fresh air.

In 1933, under the direction of Bishop Joseph G. Pinten, alterations were made in the east wing and additions were made to the faculty so that a two-year course in philosophy would follow the six-year classical program. Philosophy courses were added in order to save money during the height of the Great Depression. In 1938 the philosophy course was discontinued and the seminary returned to the six-year program of studies.

The east wing of the third floor was for fifth and sixth year students with a huge open area for recreational use. In 1942 seniors were allowed to use the pool table on the third floor every day instead of only two days a week. They were also allowed to use the new radio on the third floor at certain periods. [286] This changed in the fall of 1943 when the space was divided up with temporary partitions and double bunk beds were added to accommodate the increased enrollments. These spaces were called corrals. [287]

In 1946, first year students totaled 75 and so the burgeoning enrollment required additional sleeping space. Fr. Edmund F. Falicki, [288] on staff since his ordination in 1930, had been appointed rector earlier that year to succeed Thomas Noa, who became a bishop. Fr. Falicki guided the construction of a fourth floor, not on top of the structure but within the vast space on the third floor between the ceiling and the roof. A stairway was added along with bathrooms and showers. It was not completed until December so some students slept in the gym in the basement. [289]

Fr. John Thome recalled the changes in the main building in 1957-58. A wing was added to the chapel for the residents of St. Henry's (the Senior Department). The kitchen was enlarged and modernized. The refectory was moved from the northeast corner of the basement to south of the kitchen in the basement under the new chapel wing. At the same time stairwells were added to the southeast and southwest corners of the building to provide adequate exit in case of emergencies. In the summer of 1964, the main building "was remodeled to meet requirements of the fire marshal". Some areas received new plaster and paint. [290] This is probably when the interior stairwell was enclosed.

In 1928 excavation began for a "root cellar" behind the seminary's left wing. Dimensions were 49' 8" by 30' 2". Walls were one foot thick concrete. The roof was a reinforced concrete slab seven inches thick. [291] Fr. Thome did not recall this construction at all.

In 1954-55 George Brew was in his sixth year as janitor. [292]

Garage

In the winter of 1928-29 a new ten car garage was built. The old garage was converted to a tool shed. In early 1932, Fr. Falicki's new Oldsmobile filled the tenth spot. [293]

Convent

In the early days of the seminary, the Sisters of Mercy provided food services and lived on the first floor of the main building. In 1930 the Dominican Sisters of Marywood replaced them. [294]

With increasing enrollment and the need for more space for student and faculty needs, a convent was built for the sisters in 1948 to the east of the main building. There was a tunnel directly from the convent into the kitchen area. This building and tunnel were off limits to students.

Activities Building

South of the service entrance, along Union Boulevard, ground was broken for a new Activities Building on June 26, 1955. It was dedicated on

November 11, 1956 by Bishop Allen J. Babcock. [295] The building had three regulation basketball courts which, in season, could be converted into five volleyball courts. At the north end of the gymnasium were doors leading to four indoor handball courts. East of the gymnasium were an adjoining wing containing locker and shower rooms, a room for drying clothes, and a director's office. The exterior of the building provided wall space for ten handball courts.

College Building (St. Henry's Hall)

St. Henry's Hall 1958

Groundbreaking ceremonies for a new college building were held on March 11, 1956. [296] The sixth class moved into St. Henry's Hall, named in honor of the first bishop of the Diocese of Grand Rapids, on Good Friday, 1957. [297] It was dedicated on October 13, 1957, by Bishop Allen J. Babcock.[298] Located at the east end of the seminary drive, the building was an F-shaped structure consisting of 66 student rooms, six faculty suites, four classrooms, library, recreation room, and physics laboratory. It had a chapel on the second floor for private prayer. The students continue to gather with the rest of the seminarians in the main chapel for community prayer.

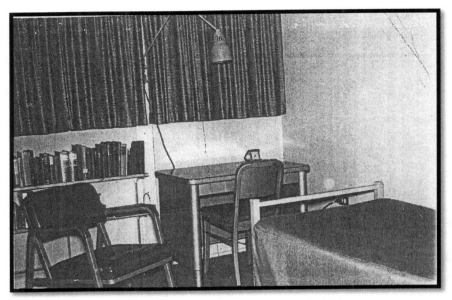

Student Residence Room in St. Henry's 1958

Classroom Wing of St. Henry's Hall

St. Henry's was only half the building planned. There was to be a mirror image hall east of St. Henry's that would double the number of residence rooms, classrooms and faculty suites. The expansion never happened, of course, because of the precipitous decline in enrollment beginning in the mid-1960's. [299]

In 1929 the seminary assets included the newly completed ten car garage. Along with other assets including bonds and donated real estate, the seminary had a value of $509,593.98.[300]

Cost in 1955-56

In 1925-26 board and tuition for students of the Diocese of Grand Rapids were $125.00 per semester. This cost was still at that level in 1956-57. The Diocese subsidized the seminary to keep the cost as low as possible. Students from other dioceses paid $300.00 per semester in 1955-56. Even this was probably not the full cost.

In addition there were fees paid by all students per semester. In 1955-56 these were:

Administration $ 3.00
Athletic $ 2.00
Science Laboratory $2.00
Library $ 3.00
Locker $ 1.00
Student Organization $ 1.00
Student Paper $ 1.00

Books, stationery, and other articles needed by the students could be procured at current prices at the Seminary store. Secondhand books were often available. Some books could be rented for a nominal fee. It is estimated that the initial expenses of a newly enrolled student for books, stationery, subscriptions, and fees was about $40.00.

Aerial View 1959

4 Transformation of St. Joseph's Seminary

St. Joseph's Seminary changed dramatically when the college students moved to Christopher House, a residence near Aquinas College, in 1969 and took classes at Aquinas College. Msgr. James P. Moran continued as rector through this change until December, 1974 when Very Rev. Anthony C. Vainavicz was appointed rector. In less than two years Very Rev. Theodore J. Kozlowski was appointed rector on June 9, 1976. His role was diminished with the appointment of Rev. James Kowalski as principal of the high school. St. Joseph's Seminary then was only a high school.

High School

St. Joseph's continued to be an on-site high school until 1981 with the primary focus being the training of young boys for the priesthood, but enrollment continued to decline. Students continued the involvement in the community which began in the 1960's.

In 1973 Bishop Joseph M. Breitenbeck commissioned a study to find alternate uses for the buildings at St. Joseph's Seminary. Shortly after that study, the students all moved to St. Henry's as their residence, but continued to use the refectory and chapel in the main building, leaving most of the main building available for other uses. St. Joseph's began to look more like a regular high school by adding a yearbook and obtaining class rings.

The next big change occurred in 1978 when students began to take classes at Catholic Central High School at 319 Sheldon Ave. SE. while retaining residence at St. Henry's. Every morning they boarded the Madison NO. 3 city bus and went to Catholic Central. Then they returned to St. Henry's after their class day ended. Priests were still in residence at St. Henry's, including Fr. James Kowalski as principal, and met with these young boys to help them determine their life vocation. While still emphasizing priesthood, the boys were made aware of other possibilities. They paid $480 in room and board at the Seminary and $700 for tuition at Catholic Central.[301] This amount was only a portion of the total $2,000 cost per students. [302]

Interestingly, St. Joseph's Seminary began in1909 with students taking some classes next door at Catholic Central "under the Sisters" [303] until 1919 when the new site was being prepared at 600 Burton St. So in one sense the seminary made a full circle. Not only were classes being taken at Catholic Central but other school activities were made available to the students at St. Joseph's.

Fr. Kowalski was hopeful that the opportunity to play sports and become involved in other extra- curricular activities would give the students a "more realistic view of the world around them".

Fr. Kowalski said the role of St. Joseph's was to "prepare young men of high school age to seek out their vocation in life." In this search programs offered at St. Joseph's were "directed to an inquiry into but are not designed to that end alone". To aid in this search there was a nightly curfew (between 9:30 p. m. and 11:30 p.m. depending on which class a student was in.

Unfortunately Fr. Kowalski's hopes were not fulfilled. In 1980-81 there were only 29 students in the four grades and only four of them were from the metropolitan area. The rest were from areas throughout the 11 county diocese. [304]

After observing the changes made for three years, a diocesan funds evaluations committee, made up of two priests and six lay persons recommended in February 1981 that the high school program be dropped in June 1981. [305]

Accordingly in March 1981 Bishop Breitenbeck informed the 29 students of the decision to close the residential school. Needless to say, the students were not happy with the decision. Meetings were held with parents and seniors were given the opportunity to finish their high school studies at Catholic Central.

The diocese continued to operate Christopher House for college seminarians [306] for about ten years. Then college seminarians were housed in different locations until July 2, 2003.

Diocesan Center

After the study in 1973 to consider converting seminary buildings to other uses, the main building was gradually occupied by diocesan offices. The religious education department of the Diocese and the bookstore were in the old study hall. There were several different offices in the old infirmary. The *Western Michigan Catholic* newspaper was in the former chemistry lab on the second floor, and the professors' suites all became various offices. The Diocesan Archives had occupied the locker rooms on the third floor from about May 1970, when 34 file cabinets of sooty, dusty correspondence were moved out to the Seminary from the chancery downtown. Those same file cabinets and much, much more were all there until the summer of 2008, when the property was sold.

In 1981 more diocesan offices moved into the vacant spaces. St. Henry's was opened as a Conference Center. In 2001 St. Henry's Hall was renovated and renamed St. Henry Spirituality & Ministry Center. At that time a chapel was added and the main entrance was located at the east end of the building, a reception area, and a parking lot. It had its own address at 660 Burton St. SE.

Grand Rapids Ellington Academy of the Arts and Technology

In August 2005, soon after Walter Hurley became the Bishop of Grand Rapids, he said that the property at 600 Burton Street was two to three times as much space as the diocese needed and announced his desire to move the diocesan offices to a more centralized location near St. Andrew's Cathedral. In early 2008 Bishop Hurley unveiled his plans for a $22 million Cathedral Square at Wealthy Street and South Division Avenue [307] and put the Burton Street property up for sale.

Marvin Sapp, a six-time Grammy Award nominee, and his wife, Malinda, were pastors of the Lighthouse Full Life Center Church on Madison St. S. E. in Grand Rapids when they looked longingly at the property at 600 Burton St. "We'd drive by it all the time and say, 'Man, wouldn't it be great to acquire this property to do this ministry?'" Marvin Sapp said. [308]

After getting approval from the board at Lighthouse Church,[309] the Sapps made an offer to the Diocese. A deal was made but then a problem arose and the deal was called off. Within a few days, the sale was back on and the Sapps purchased the 17 acre property for $3.3 million in March 2008.

The Sapps originally called the property Kingdom Square where they planned to use current space for a ministry center and eventually build a new church in the southeast corner. [3]But the Sapps wanted to do more than find a larger location for their ministry. "When Marvin and I attended the Grand Rapids schools, our teachers told us that one day when we are successful, we would have an obligation to give back to the schools," Malinda Sapp said. [310]

Initially the Sapps considered the Grand Rapids Public School pilot program, Centers of Innovation. Ultimately they established a performing arts center called the Ellington Academy of Arts and Technology, named for the jazz legend Duke Ellington and modeled after the Winans Academy of Performing Arts in Detroit. Sapp said the vision was to incorporate the study of performing arts and technology into the traditional core curriculum to increase critical thinking and academic skills. The school would require parental involvement and uniforms and feature a Spanish language curriculum." [311]

Bishop Hurley said about the plans the Sapps were making at the time of the sale: "I think it's wonderful what they want to do here. It's consistent

---

[3] A ministry center is no longer part of the plan.

with what the mission of this place has been over the years. We like to think God's at work in ways we don't always understand." [312]

In 2009, more than 100 students in grades 2–12 enrolled in Ellington Academy's after-school extended day learning program. In 2011 GREAAT Schools, Inc. was awarded a Michigan Department of Education Charter School Planning and Implementation Grant. In 2012 Lake Superior State University approved the charter for the Grand Rapids Ellington Academy of Arts and Technology.

The school was launched at the Burton Street location in the fall 2012 with 161 middle school students in 6th - 8th grade. In 2013 the Academy expanded to include daytime classes for Pre-K to 5th Grade with a total enrollment of 370 students. In 2013-14, 377 students enrolled in the Ellington Academy, grades pre-K-9th. In 2014-15 the enrollment was 330 through tenth grade plus 12-16 additional pre-school students. . Each year, the Academy will add a grade level until the 12th grade class of 2017 graduates.

For the 2015-16 school year, the projected enrollment is about 300 students from pre-K through 11th grade. The 12th grade will be added in 2016-17. This total is intentionally lower than the previous year so the staff can concentrate on academic excellence and to build on the successes of the previous years.

Unfortunately, Malinda Sapp will not be sharing in the planning and administration of the Academy as she died September 9, 2010, from complications of colon cancer. [313]

The Grand Rapids YMCA partnered with Ellington Academy Pre-K Program to establish Ellington Pre-K Academy. The Pre-K Academy is currently rated as a five-star preschool.

Elementary students currently use the first floor in the former St. Henry's Hall. The other grades meet in 16 modular classrooms until the renovation of the main building is completed where all grades will have classes. The middle school and high school offices are already in the main building while the administration offices are in the former convent.

Renovation of the Academic Building (main building) is expected to cost $5.9 million providing for 27+ classroom spaces, four science lab spaces, student commons spaces, and performing arts spaces for creative arts, theatrical arts, musical arts, and technology media cafe and literacy center. This cost also includes additional upgrades to HVAC, athletic center, and outside features for student learning and play, including an amphitheater (new building) and new playground.

Future plans also include a Performing Arts Building in memory of Dr. Malinda P. Sapp. It will feature main stage theatre, world languages, performance and lab space for small groups, commons space. This is a few years distant but pl

Ellington Academy will use St. Henry's Hall as conference space for over-night accommodations for 60 hotel spaces and have full commercial kitchen facilities.

Epilogue

My Class of 1961 has held many reunions over the years. They weren't in five year or ten year intervals, like organized classes seem to have, but rather we had one when some classmates took on the challenge to invite the class to a gathering of some kind. We did however have a twentieth year class reunion in 1981. Many contributed to the success of these reunions but Bob Lesinski and Paul Kress were two key people for many of them.

I believe we had reunions in 1974, 1977, 1981, 1994, and 2007.More recently we have decided to have a reunion every two years beginning in 2012. These reunions are open to anyone who was ever a member of our class. We don't have a lot of guys attend and we don't even have contact information for many of them. But there are about 20 who are very interested in getting together because we established a camaraderie and friendship so many years ago that are still with us, even though in many cases we haven't seen each other during most of our working years except perhaps at one or two reunions.

The 1981 reunion involved a gathering at St. Henry's on Friday evening, a family picnic at the seminary on Saturday morning, and festive meal Saturday evening. We marveled at each other and our experiences at this place. We wanted to go inside the main building but it was locked. Someone noticed a window open on the third floor and sent his son up the fire escape. The boy entered the building, came down to the main entrance, and let us in. We walked around showing off the place to our wives and children. We even met a priest there but he didn't ask why we were in the building or how we got in!

This reunion was at a hotel in Grand Rapids. We were to meet at a certain room to register. I was walking outside toward the door and I heard someone inside say, "Surely he is not one of ours." I had turned gray already and they didn't recognize me. This was also the one at which several of us were "kicked out" of our room for being too noisy but the hotel allowed us to sit on the floor in a secluded space, drink beer or wine, and tell stories. We all laughed so much that night that we ached. The next day no one could recall what was so funny.

The 1994 reunion was the largest one and it was held in the main building. Unfortunately I was unable to stay for all of it.

Bob Lesinski organized an all seminary reunion in 2007. He put together a video presentation of slides and music taped at the seminary. I doubt there was a dry eye when we got to the end of that show. You can see it on YouTube. See links on page 2.

I organized and invited classmates to come to a reunion in 2012 and 2014 with another one coming up in 2016. The men attending discovered that the camaraderie is still there. We had a unique experience at St. Joe's that cannot be duplicated today because the times and the Church are different.

There was a time when I had very negative feelings about my experience at St. Joe's but I have come to relish the good times and good friends much more. One of the Promises in AA is "We will not regret the past nor wish to shut the door on it". That sums up precisely how I feel about St. Joe's.

Appendix A: The Rule

Students were given a hint at what the life in the seminary would be in the annual bulletin for the school but the details were contained in a book called *The Rule of St. Joseph's Seminary*. I have included it here verbatim. After St. Henry's Hall was opened, rules were added for the particular circumstances surrounding that facility and the relationship between students in the two buildings. .

Part I was about the seminary and what it meant to be a seminarian and an aspirant to the most holy calling of being a priest. Part II then fully elaborated on the training of a seminarian. Here is where all the rules were carefully spelled out. These statements included such things as spiritual exercises and prayers, but also minute details about obedience to the rules and to our superiors.

There is a nuance of meaning in the title of this little book which I missed when I was a seminarian. It doesn't say "Rules" (plural) but Rule (singular) implying that it was intended to be a way of life, as in "the rule of St. Benedict". The first part of this book makes that very clear. The specific rules in the second part, however, were what many of us students focused on rather than the way of life that was intended.

This way of life involved several areas of life, each to be fully accepted and encouraged. These were prayer, study, recreation, and rest, along with personal responsibilities. Food was provided but even there we had kitchen duties from time to time. .

The Rule of St. Joseph's Seminary

Part I TheSeminary and the Seminarian

SECTION I - Purpose of the Seminary

St. Joseph's Seminary has for its sole purpose the training of young aspirants to the holy priesthood. The course of studies covers a period of six years and aims to give the student that intellectual enlargement that will serve as a solid foundation for his higher studies.

Simultaneously with the acquisition of knowledge and the development of the intellectual faculties there must be a sound growth in virtue and piety, and a real upbuilding of moral character. The aspirant to Christ's priesthood must learn from his early years to know and follow his Divine Master. Hence the Seminary must be a second Nazareth, a retreat removed from the distractions of the world, where Christ's chosen ones may hearken to that voice which teaches the lessons of the Hidden Life.

The specific work of the Seminary has been sufficiently defined by the Church and, in particular, by the Council of Trent, the Plenary Councils of Baltimore, and more recently by the new Code of Canon Law. It is the endeavor of this institution to follow these prescriptions as closely as possible.

SECTION II - The Priestly Vocation

1. Vocation. The priestly vocation is essentially a call to accept the priesthood, extended to a man in God's name by the legitimate ministers of the Church. There are two elements in vocation, namely, the free selection and call given by the Bishop whereby he invites a suitable man to enter the priestly state, and the conferring of Holy Orders upon this man. No one enters the Seminary already possessing a vocation. The aspirant to the priesthood enters the Seminary in order that, by the aid of the grace of God, he may acquire that suitability which the Church and the Bishop require for the call given to him, and that he may acquire and develop the right intention to freely accept the call.

2. Intention and Suitability. The aspirant to the priesthood must have a sincere intention to become a priest, an intention that comes by God's grace from prayer, serious reflection, and is made firm by cooperation with God's gifts and graces. This intention plays an important part in the acquisition of suitability. Suitability is based on the gifts of nature and grace, and is shown by such

righteousness of life and sufficiency of knowledge as will give a well-founded hope that the aspirant will perform the duties of the priestly state properly and fulfill its obligations worthily. In other words, this development of the moral and intellectual life must be such as indicates that the aspirant is developing the habit of self-control (*disciplina*), through which, by the aid of the rule, he shows clearly a personal guidance and control over his own moral and intellectual life so that he will seem "not merely fashioned to this holy tenor of life, but born to it."

This suitability is ascertained by the Seminary authorities in the name of the Bishop. The proof of its possession is to be found in a definite and positive development of virtue and of character, and in progress towards a certain standard of knowledge. Obedience, piety, humility, fidelity to rules, and an upright intention are virtues that are necessary in an aspirant to the priesthood. He must have reverence for sacred things, and zeal for the glory of God. Exceptional ability in studies is not necessary, but sufficient mental talents to reach a certain standard of knowledge are required. Evidence of good judgment in keeping with the candidate's age is indispensable. The mark of the Christian gentleman must be in evidence.

The sincerity and firmness of the seminarian's intention to become a priest are measured and tested by the progress he makes in the development of these gifts of grace and of nature.

The seminary authorities are interested principally in developing the positive traits of the candidates for the priesthood. They may not, however, fail to recognize evidence of unsuitability. In accordance with Church law then: "Disorderly, incorrigible, or seditious students, and those who because of their character or temperament do not seem suitable candidates for the clerical state, shall be dismissed from the seminary. Students who progress so slowly in their studies that there is not much hope that they will acquire sufficient learning, shall also be dismissed. If a seminarian should be guilty of an offense against good morals or the faith, he shall be summarily discharged." (Canon 1371)

Though rashness in entering the sanctuary is gravely reprehensible, undue concern about one's fitness should also be avoided. The seminarian must strive to acquire a persevering spirit of humility; this, together with purity of intention in devoting himself wholly to the service of God, is all that is required. And the grace of God will not be wanting.

3. The Teaching of the Church. The mind of the Church is clear concerning the priestly vocation. A special 'commission of Cardinals appointed by Pope Pius X to examine this question as expounded by Canon Joseph Lahitton in one of his books pronounced the following judgment:

"The work of Canon Joseph Lahitton entitled 'The Priestly Vocation' is on no account to be condemned. Nay, more, in so far as it contains the three following propositions, it is to be very specially commended. The propositions are:

"1. No one has ever any right to ordination prior to his free selection by the Bishop.

"2. That requisite on the part of the candidate for Orders which is called priestly vocation does not by any means consist (at least necessarily and ordinarily) in a certain interior attraction of the subject or in invitations of the Holy Spirit to enter the priesthood.

"3. On the contrary, in order that one may be rightly called by the Bishop, nothing further is required beyond right intention, together with that suitability which is based on such gifts of nature and grace and which is proved by such probity of life and sufficiency of knowledge as will give a well-founded hope that he will be able to discharge the duties of the priestly state properly and fulfill the obligations of that state in a holy manner.

"His Holiness, Pius X, in an audience granted on June 26th, has fully approved of their Eminences' decision."- (Acta Ap. Sed., Vol. IV, p. 485, A. D. 1912)

SECTION III - Admission of Students

1. Only students who have the intention of preparing themselves for the priesthood and who give good hope of acquiring suitability for a vocation shall be admitted and allowed to remain.

2. A student seeking admission to the Seminary shall be furnished with a form for his personal application. A special recommendation blank shall be filled out by the applicant's pastor and sent as a confidential communication to the Rector. Students who have attended another Seminary or boarding school must also present a testimonial letter from that institution.

3. All applicants must be in sound health and free from - canonical impediments.

4. All applicants must have satisfactorily completed the eighth grade.

It is advised that boys aspiring to the priesthood enter the Seminary High School at the completion of their eighth grade. The applicants should present a report card which will show at least a C or 78 average in elementary English, arithmetic, and social studies.

While the Seminary is desirous of recognizing credits obtained above the grammar grades, it finds it necessary, in keeping with the requirements of Major Seminaries, to maintain high standards. Accordingly applicants for higher grades in high school are required to pass a satisfactory examination especially in Latin. Experience has shown that most of those who make their high school course before enrolling in the Seminary must attend special classes for one or more years, before they are adequately adjusted to a prescribed course of studies.

5. The Rector and the Superiors will judge about the student's fitness for admission and continuation.

It is a mistaken notion, entertained by some, that the age of thirteen or fourteen is too early for a boy to begin his studies for the priesthood. Centuries of experience have shown that opinion to be false.

Part II THE TRAINING OF THE SEMINARIAN

SECTION I - The Spirit of the Seminary

"Put ye on the Lord Jesus Christ." (Rom. XIII-14)

The priest is called by God to carry on the work of Jesus Christ. As an *allter Christus* he must follow in the footsteps of the Divine Model who taught first by example, then by words: "Jesus began to do and to teach." (Acts 1-1). The constant solicitude of the Church in regard to seminarians is that Christ be formed in them, and thus they may prepare themselves to carry on Christ's work.

Therefore, all seminarians must aspire, first of all, to personal holiness and sanctity through prayer, self-denial, and the use of the Sacraments. Next, the seminarian must study with perseverance to acquire that learning and culture which is required for his work as teacher, and to adorn his person with that quality of dignified and Christian gentlemanliness of manner in the absence of which his work would be less effective.

This cannot be done unless there is order and discipline in the life of the seminarian. The daily programs of spiritual exercises, study, and recreation is intended as an aid to the acquisition of holiness, learning, gentlemanliness, and the habit of self-discipline. This program has real value only insofar as it instills in the seminarian the habit of using his talents, abilities, and time to train himself, so that the priestly character of holiness, learning, and gentlemanliness shall seem to be not merely fashioned but born in him. It is only thus that he will learn how "to do and to teach."

In the Seminary the student undergoes the traditional training that has formed holy and saintly priests. All the incidents of his daily life are a part of his training. To neglect or to put aside any of the rules and regulations deliberately is to put aside a part of that training with its corresponding means of sanctification. It is a sin against obedience to violate the Seminary rules in grave matters or with a persistence that causes grave results in the house. The candidate for the holy priesthood must take a high view of the rules of the Seminary, even at an early age. They do not destroy his liberty, but deepen his purity of heart, and tend to his personal well-being.

"Those students will conduct themselves in the priesthood in a perfect and holy manner, who have cultivated the virtues of this state from their boyhood and have so far progressed in their self-control (disciplina) that they seem not merely fashioned to this holy tenor of life, but born to it." (Leo XIII., Encl. "Etsi Nos," 'February 15th, 1882.)

"The lack of these virtues (obedience, piety, humility, fidelity to rules, upright intention, virtues which the Pope declares necessary for seminarians) will soon betray itself where the religious exercises are performed in a spirit of hypocrisy, and where the discipline is observed not by the voice of conscience, but by reason of fear. He who keeps the discipline by servile fear or violates it through levity of mind and contempt, is very far from giving any hope of worthily performing the priestly duties. It is hard to believe that he who despises the discipline of the house, will not break away from the public laws of the Church." (Pius X, Motu Proprio, September 1, 1910.)

SECTION II - Spiritual Exercises

1. Ordinary Christian virtue does not suffice for the priest. By the dignity of his sacred calling he is bound to strive for greater virtue and personal holiness. The love of piety and an earnest effort to advance therein, are signs of the priestly vocation in a boy. There is nothing wonderful in asking a candidate for the priesthood to strengthen that foundation of true holiness at an early age. The sanctification of a seminarian is effected by his daily work and by his religious exercises, but primarily by the latter. The regular practice of these religious exercises is an absolute necessity, if he is to prepare himself for the priestly life. The various exercises

prescribed by the Seminary order are few and brief; a well-disposed seminarian will seek time and opportunity to increase them. It is, however, of more importance to perform the few exercises with care than to enlarge their number and fail in their performance.

2. A spirit of deep reverence, faith; and devotion should characterize the performance of all spiritual exercises. The sacred ceremonies and chants of the liturgy shall be carried out with precision and decorum. All vocal prayers shall be recited with a distinct, clear, and well modulated voice.

3. Daily exercises in the community:

Morning prayers and meditation.

Holy Mass.

Visit to the Blessed Sacrament.

Rosary.

Spiritual reading.

Night prayers; examination of conscience.

Frequent and daily Holy Communion is essential for a seminarian. In the frequent reception of the Holy Eucharist he must guard himself against routine by devoting a set space of time to preparation and thanksgiving, and by using various Communion devotions.

4. Weekly Devotions.

a. Confession. Every student must each week present himself to his confessor, unless he has been advised differently by his spiritual director. Ordinary and extraordinary confessors are appointed to hear' confessions. Priests on the Seminary faculty may be extraordinary confessors. A student may freely ask for any priest outside of the Seminary.

b. On Sundays and Holydays of obligation the students shall take part in all the sacred offices of the church - Solemn Mass, Vespers, and Benediction of the Blessed Sacrament.

c. Every Sunday all students shall attend a Spiritual . Conference in which the principles and ideals of the priesthood are presented and explained.

d. Every Saturday evening there is Benediction and the singing of the Litany of the Blessed Virgin.

5. Special Devotions.

The students shall faithfully assist at all special devotions held during the course of the year, as set forth in the manual "Prayers and Devotions."

These special devotions are as follows:

The Annual Retreat.

The Monthly Day of Recollection.

Benediction of the Blessed Sacrament on days appointed.

First Friday. Month of October.

Novena for the Immaculate Conception. The Chair of Unity Octave.

Month of March.

Novena for Vocations.

Way of the Cross.

Month of May.

Novena for Pentecost.

Novena of the Sacred Heart.

Six Sundays of St. Aloysius.

SECTION III - Rules of Discipline and Order.

Article 1 – The Spirit of Discipline

A seminarian is naturally expected to be actuated by the noblest motives that a delicate conscience and the sense of honor inspire. Other motives to spur him on to the fulfillment of his duties come into play only in as far as the unstable nature of youth demands them as supports. The Seminary affords growing boys the same protection that they receive in their well-conducted parental homes; the supervision of parents is replaced by that of the Seminary authorities. Their direction does not confine itself to general counsels or commands, but gives individual attention to the students. The nature of a large community and the definite plan of training imposes duties to which the student freely submits as soon as he asks to be admitted to the Seminary. In their main outlines these duties demand from the student the spirit of obedience and mortification, and the love of order and punctuality.

A well behaved seminarian will never deliberately and of set purpose break the rules. Failings through thoughtlessness, or in the weakness of the moment, may be excused. He who frequently fails in his work or evades it when he conveniently can, who is slack and unpunctual, or wastes his time, will never make up for the training he has missed, nor will he obtain the graces that would have been his had he made faithful use of the means that God gave him to obtain them.

Article 2 - Superiors

1. The principle of authority stands foremost in the Seminary. The student must feel and show a sincere and manly respect and a

spirit of obedience to Superiors and professors. He should aim at being truthful and candid with them. He who is insubordinate, or incites and promotes a spirit of insubordination shall not be allowed to remain.

2. The students shall have free access to the Superiors at all times. In asking for anything they must exercise becoming courtesy and deference to the Superior's will.

3. The students have no right to demand the reason of a Superior's decision; circumstances may not permit the Superior to make known the reason.

4. Some students are appointed prefects and are charged with certain responsibilities in disciplinary matters. They are to be respected and obeyed as representatives of authority. They shall report all infractions of discipline to the Superiors.

5. No student shall use a permission obtained from his Superior without notifying his immediate disciplinary official of the grant of the permission.

Article 3 - Community Life

1. A spirit of brotherly love and good fellowship should rule in the community.

2. Every seminarian exercises an influence over his fellow students. Let him beware of the warning of our Lord, lest he become a scandal-giver. Let him remember that it is a serious matter to lessen the ideals of the priestly calling in his companion. If he loves and spreads worldly ideas that should remain foreign to the ambassador of Christ, he shows thereby that he is out of place in the Seminary.

3. The spirit of disobedience and discontent is very contagious in community life. One grumbler can affect many. The seminarian will refrain from fault-finding and criticism. He owes a duty to the Seminary and to the vocation to which he aspires to set up a high ideal for himself which will spread itself to others and be a good influence on the whole spirit of the community.

4. The seminarian must exercise Christian gentlemanliness and good manners towards all in word and action. Polite manners should regulate his conduct at the table, at study, in the chapel, on the campus, and wheresoever he meets his fellowman. He may not be a stranger to the proper forms of polite society. Not only the sense of politeness but the sense of justice will tell the seminarian that he may never selfishly take more than his share of what is set out for all.

5. In their mutual relations seminarians shall not align themselves into cliques, nor maintain exclusive private friendships.

6. Association between students of the higher classes and younger students is forbidden.

7. All hatreds, discords, and dissensions should be banished from the Seminary. The cause of dissension shall be removed at once.

8. Slang, vulgar and unbecoming language, uncharitable bantering, the use of insulting epithets or improper nicknames shall not be tolerated. It is self-evident that no one shall offer physical violence to another.

9. The student shall carefully refrain from meddling in the affairs of others, but if.he have a certain knowledge of matters of grave importance which may be a source of scandal to others and may injure the reputation of the Seminary, he is in conscience bound to consult his spiritual director as to what steps to take.

10. No student may open the desk or locker of another, nor in any way molest another's belongings.

11. Certain students are appointed as prefects and to other offices. As such, they occupy positions of trust in the community and should be accorded proper consideration. All students must cooperate with them, and thus learn the lesson of responsibility.

12. Every student is expected to engage cheerfully and willingly in any work, manual or otherwise, that his Superiors may ask him to perform. The call to the priesthood implies service, a life-long sacrifice of self to the interests of others. The seminarian must seek every occasion of service that promotes forgetfulness of self. No student must think that he has done his whole duty by merely attending to his own personal studies and duties. He must seek opportunities to serve the community and others.

13. The students shall exhibit proper deference and respect to the Sisters. They are forbidden to place any commissions with the Sisters. They shall not hold long conversations with any person employed by the Seminary nor use them as agents in any capacity.

14. The collection of money or the exercise of any agency in the Seminary is forbidden.

15. The lending or borrowing of money and the exchange of personal effects is not permitted. The students are forbidden to have any charge accounts with merchants or professional people.

Article 4 - Punctuality

1. The good order of the house demands that all students be punctual at the summons to duty. The habit of punctuality is a requisite for efficiency in work.

2. At the second sound of the bell all students shall be in their places and in silence wait for whatever exercise is on the program.

3. At the appointed hour all students shall promptly retire, and shall promptly arise at the sound of the bell.

4. Tardiness or absence from any spiritual exercise, class or study period, must be reported at once to the proper authority.

Article 5 - Silence

1. The daily order in the Seminary demands that silence be maintained except during recreation.

2. Strict silence is observed from night prayers until breakfast the following morning.

3. During study hours strict silence must be kept in the study hall, wash rooms, corridors, and at all times in the sacristy, library and reading rooms.

4. Silence is also to be observed during the following periods:
At the second sound of the bell for chapel or refectory.
During reading in the refectory.

5. During the Forty Hours' Adoration and during the last three days of Holy Week the students shall refrain from all loud talking, noisy mirth, playing of musical instruments, and such games as would disturb the religious calm required for those days of worship.

6. Strict silence is observed during the annual retreat, the monthly day of recollection, and during the observance of the Tre Ore on Good Friday.

7. Loud and boisterous talking as well as running and scuffling are forbidden at all times in the corridors, study hall, class-rooms, and dormitories.

Article 6 - Building and Grounds

1. No student shall leave the Seminary grounds except by permission of the Rector. The Rector reserves to himself the granting of this permission.

2. The student shall use his permission to visit only those persons or places expressed in the permission. He shall report to the proper authority immediately upon his return.

3. Normally, students shall not receive permission to leave the Seminary grounds with visitors.

4. Unauthorized absence from the seminary is a serious offense punishable by dismissal.

5. The prescribed limits on the grounds must be strictly observed.

6. There are certain parts of the building that students may not enter, other parts only at certain times.

a. The dormitories may be entered in the evening before retiring, in the morning after breakfast. They are also open during recreation hours for a change of clothes for games.

b. The refectory may be entered only during meal time, and the infirmary during the recreation period after supper for the purpose of medical aid.

c. Classrooms may be used outside of study hours for speech or music practice. At no time, however, may a student lock the room or bar entrance to others.

d. It is forbidden for students of one department to enter those parts of the building which are reserved to the other department, or any other part where duty does not call them.

6. It is strictly forbidden for a student of the senior department to enter the room of another student.

7. It is strictly forbidden to use or to have in possession tobacco in any form.

Article 7 - Neatness and Cleanliness

1. Personal Cleanliness. The dress of the seminarian shall be plain and sober. Hence colored ties, hats and suits, and all extreme and worldly fashions must be avoided. Every student will endeavor to be neat and clean, particularly for divine services, for meals, and for class time. But the care of the person should never take the form of the foolish vanities of the fop. Wordly fashions in dress, in the care of the hair, and the use of jewelry and of perfumes must be avoided. On the other hand, the seminarian must not be slovenly and careless in his personal appearance; let him ever be guided by the spirit of his calling and the dictates of common sense.

2. Cleanliness in the Building.

a. Waste paper and other refuse is to be placed in the receptacles provided for such purpose. The toilet and shower rooms must be kept clean, and each student must cooperate to keep them in this condition.

b. No substance, such as writing paper, soap wrappers, apple cores, etc., that would in any way interfere with the drainage, must ever be thrown into any of the drains of these rooms.

c. Great care must be exercised in the refectory so that the tables will be kept clean. Proper table etiquette is to be observed always and the student's behavior at the table must be that of the gentleman.

d. It is not permitted to keep or eat food above the basement floor. The chewing of gum is forbidden.

e. Students are held responsible for the use and care, of Seminary property. Any student who damages Seminary property, even accidentally, shall at once report the matter to the Rector.

f. It is forbidden to deface doors, windows, or any piece of furniture by writing, scratching, or by cutting figures and lines on them. Care must be taken not to soil the walls or floors.

3. Dormitories and Rooms.

a. Each student must keep his bed and surroundings in perfect condition. Regulations concerning various appointments in the rooms must be strictly followed. .

b. All clothing and other articles must be kept in the lockers.

c. On rising, each student shall fold back his bedding over the foot of the bed, keeping it off the floor. Immediately after breakfast he shall arrange his bed carefully and neatly. This must not be done before breakfast.

d. Beds and stands must be left in the position in which they have been set. It is forbidden to sit on beds when made, or to use them for resting during the day.

4. Study-Hall.

a. Books and stationery must be kept in order. Only articles pertaining to study or correspondence may be kept in the desk.

b. The bulletin board and chalk boards shall be used for official business only; extraneous news and frivolous matters shall not be displayed.

Article 8 -' Correspondence

1. The Rector reserves to himself the right to inspect all mail, telegrams, and parcels addressed to students or sent out by them. All letters and parcels for mailing must pass through the regular Seminary mail-box.

2. No student may subscribe for or receive newspapers or periodicals.

3. It is forbidden to write articles or communications of any kind for publication.

4. Correspondence not in keeping with the character of candidates for the priesthood is not allowed.

No student is allowed to act in the capacity of agent.

Boxes containing provisions are not permitted to be brought in or sent in by mail.

Article 9 - Visitors

1. Regular visits of parents and relatives are allowed on the days and during the hours appointed.

2. Except on open house days, visitors will be received only in the reception rooms.

3. Visits from persons other than parents or relatives may be allowed by special permission. Visits from dismissed students are not permitted.

4. No student shall be called to the telephone except at the discretion of the Rector. Only the most necessary and urgent calls will be heeded.

Article 10 - Recreation

1. All students should enter wholeheartedly into the common recreations of the Seminary. They must not seek exclusion or refuse to fraternize with all. They should seek to make themselves a part of all activities.

2. All students, unless excused, shall take part in outdoor recreation during certain periods each day. Every student should take part with a good will in the various games promoted on the campus. Good sportsmanship in athletic contests should be the mark of every student.

3. The student should aim to enjoy the great benefit of out-of-doors walking. On certain days walks outside the grounds are permitted.

4. Students going out for a walk shall be dressed fittingly, and shall observe proper decorum in speech and in the manner of their gait, free from all vulgarity and roughness.

5. Students walk in groups, each group with a prefect.

No group of students may leave for a walk except in the presence of one of their Superiors.

During the walks no places shall be visited save the place or places approved by the Rector. It is forbidden to enter stores or places of business, or to meet anyone by appointment. The students may not separate so that they escape the observation of the prefect. No smoking is allowed during these walks. Special permission must be received for the use of any means of transportation.

6. During programs of entertainment or talks by guest speakers all students are required to be present.

SECTION IV - Rules of Study

Article 1 Study

1. There is no royal road to knowledge; all alike must travel over the same laborious way. Hard work, constant application, diligent study are indispensable means in the acquisition of learning.

2. Learning in the priesthood must go hand in hand with piety. Hence carelessness in the preparation of lessons and anything that indicates a neglect of studies is looked upon either as a sign of lack of vocation or as evidence that the student does not regard his vocation seriously.

3. Study hours are most valuable time. Each student shall devote these hours at his desk to diligent work. Letter-writing, the reading of books not connected with assigned work, and other occupations foreign to study are forbidden during the regular study hours.

During the free study hours students may occupy themselves with correspondence and reading, but this time is not to be employed in idle gazing at pictures, in making album collections, or in games.

4. The importance of honesty at all times is so evident as scarcely to require comment. If any student be found employing dishonest means in examination, such as copying from books, papers, or another's paper, or by receiving help in any way from anyone, a note to that effect shall appear on the semi-annual report. He who furnishes illegal assistance shall likewise be censured. Students are not permitted to receive assistance from their fellow-students in preparing their class work, and plagiarism of any kind shall be severely punished.

5. The student is encouraged to seek the assistance of his own teachers in all difficulties.

6. Only those textbooks are permitted for use that are approved, and these must be free from all pencil or pen notations. The use of keys, interlinear editions, and translations (printed or in manuscript) is prohibited in class.

Article 2 - Reports and Grades

1. A report of the student's progress is sent by the student to the parents at regular intervals during each semester; this report is to be signed by the parents. A semester report is also issued; an accompanying certification that the report has been examined is to be returned to the Rector with the signature of the parents and of the Pastor.

2. The students are graded as follows:

Conduct and Application: I - Good; II - Fair (Advised to improve); III - Unsatisfactory (Must Improve); IV - Poor.

Academic Grades:

A (94-100) Extraordinary;

B (86-93) Better than average;

C (78-85) Average;

D (70-77) Less than average;

F (Less than 70) Failure.

3. Low grades, lack of interest, or neglect of work during any semester renders a student liable to probation. A student who does not maintain an average higher than 78 or C will be warned. If a student's scholastic average is less than 78 or C, or if a student has one failing grade he will be put on probation for the succeeding semester. During the period of probation, the student is on trial to prove his fitness to carry a seminary course of studies. He is required to remove the probation to qualify for promotion in the course or for graduation.

Article 3 - Library and Books

1. The students are encouraged to make frequent use of the Seminary Library. The reading of books for collateral study, especially of classical authors, is an indispensable means for the acquisition of culture. Discretion is to be used in selecting books.

2. In the use of books from the library the students shall be governed by the regulations put in force by the Librarian.

3. Strict silence must be observed in the library and reading rooms at all times, and any occupation not in harmony with library work is forbidden.

4. Books and periodicals must be handled with care and after being used must be returned to their proper place. No student is allowed to set aside any article for his own exclusive use.

5. Students are not permitted to use or have in their possession textbooks not approved by their teachers. No book or periodical

shall be in the possession of the students save such as are approved by the Authorities.

6. The legislation of the Holy See regarding the reading of books, newspapers, and periodicals shall be strictly enforced.

Article 4 - Music

1. Proficiency in music is an accomplishment that offers pleasant pastime to the student and great advantages to the priest. The students should endeavor to acquire some knowledge of the principles and laws, and of the art of sacred music. The study of musical instruments is recommended and encouraged.

2. All printed music shall be submitted for approval to the proper authorities.

3. The use of the worldly music of the theater and dance hall is forbidden.

SECTION V - General Order

Article I

Daily Class Days
    A.M.
6:00-Rise
6:20-Morning Prayers Meditation
6:50-Holy Mass
7:30-Study
7: 55-Breakfast
8:45-Class
10:25-Intermission
10:30-Class
    P.M.
12:15-Visit to the Blessed Sacrament
12:20-Dinner
1:30-Class or Study
4 :00-Recreation
5:30-Study
6:30-Supper Recreation
7:30-Rosary
7:45-Spiritual Reading
7:55-Study
8:55-Benediction on appointed days
9:00-Night Prayers
9:30-Retire

Sundays
  A.M.
6:30-Rise
6:50-Morning Prayers Meditation
7:20-Holy Mass
8:00-Study
8:25-Breakfast
9:15-Solemn High Mass Recreation
11:00-Student Organizations Meetings
  P.M.
12:30-Visit to the Blessed Sacrament
12:35-Dinner
3:30- Vespers, Benediction Recreation
5:30-Conference
6:00-Supper Recreation
7:30-Rosary
7:45-Spiritual Reading
7:55-Study
9:00-Night Prayers
9:30-Retire

No classes are held on Wednesday or Saturday afternoons.
On Saturdays and holidays the students rise at 6:30. The order of the day for holidays is the same as on Sundays, except that recreation extends from breakfast until dinner. The afternoon is free until study is resumed at 5:30. Solemn High Mass on Holy Days at 9:15.
The Saturday Benediction is at 8:40.
Way of the Cross during Lent: Wednesday, 5:00; Friday, 6:15.
Monthly Day of Recollection
First Sunday of the Month 9:15---Solemn High Mass and Exposition of the Blessed Sacrament
  11:00-Conference
  12:15---Rosary
  12:30-Dinner
  2:00-Conference
  3:00-Vespers and Reposition of Blessed Sacrament

Article 2 - Schedule of Holydays and Holidays
Anniversary of Holy Father's Coronation.

108

The Most Reverend Bishop's Patron Saint's Day. Feast of All Saints.

Thanksgiving Day.

Feast of the Immaculate Conception. Christmas vacation of two weeks. Feast of St. Thomas Aquinas. Feast of St. Joseph.

Holy Thursday, Good Friday, and Holy Saturday. Easter vacation of one week.

Solemnity of St. Joseph.

Feast of the Ascension.

Field Day and Open House.

Memorial Day.

SECTION VI - Vacation

1. The students must report to the Rector before leaving the premises at the opening of vacation, and again before the hour set for the close of vacation. Students are not permitted to delay their return home for vacation unless they have received permission from the Rector.

2. During the days of vacation the seminarian must preserve the internal and external sanctity of life which his holy vocation demands, that he may give edification to the faithful and promote the honor of the Church.

3. The seminarian is forbidden to attend theaters, dances, and other worldly places of amusement. He will provide for himself safeguards against the paganism of modern literature, radio, and television. He will renounce and avoid the company of members of the other sex.

4. Every student should assist at Holy Mass daily, and should receive the Sacrament of Penance and the Eucharist as frequently as was the order of life in the Seminary. On Sundays and Holydays he should be present at all the religious functions of his parish church.

5. All preparations for the opening of the school year should be made in season; shopping, medical and dental work should be tended to before the student returns to the Seminary.

6. If for any cause a student is prevented from returning on the appointed day, he shall inform the Rector in advance, and shall bring a letter from the Pastor attesting the truth of the cause of the delay.

7. In large measure, a seminarian is the responsibility of his Pastor with whom he is advised to keep in touch throughout the vacation. In accordance with statute No. 28 of the Second Synod of Grand Rapids, the Pastor is under obligation to submit to the

Rector a signed and sealed report about the seminarian's conduct during vacation time.

Supplement to the Rule
These rules were added in the fall 1957 because of the changed conditions after St. Henry's opened for college students or as referred to here as the Senior Department. These changes are in Part II, Section III.

Article 2 Seniors
6. Students in the senior department shall be responsible for making the Rector or the Priest who is in charge during the Rector's absence aware of their own violation of the rules.

7. Each student will own a copy of the RULE of Saint Joseph's Seminary.

Article 5 Silence
1a. Even during time of recreation, silence must be kept throughout the residence hall.

Article 6 Buildings and Grounds
6e. It is strictly forbidden for a student of the senior department to enter the room of another student. To do so requires a special and most explicit permission of the Rector or of the priest who is in charge during the Rector's absence. The violation of this rule makes a student liable to dismissal.

It is forbidden to be at the door of another seminarian.

In the junior department it is strictly forbidden to use or to have in possession tobacco in any form.

In the senior department smoking is permitted only during recreation time which immediately follows the meals.

Even during times of recreation smoking is permitted only on the grounds limited by the path east of the residence hall. It is strictly forbidden to smoke in the buildings at all times. Smoking is not permitted off campus. Any violation of the rules concerning the use of tobacco makes a student liable to dismissal.

Article 7 Neatness and Cleanliness
Dormitories and Rooms
a-1. Each student shall take proper care of his own room.

a-2. No furnishings are permitted other than those supplied by the Seminary.

a-3. No one shall drive nails or tacks into the walls or attach anything to the walls.

a-4. Any damage to the room or its furnishings shall be repaired at the expense of the students.

a-5. No trunks may be taken to the student's room.

a-6. Students are forbidden to have radios. The violation of this rule is punishable by dismissal.

a-7. Rooms are inspected by a member of the Faculty at least once a week.

Article 9. Visitors

2 a. Visitors will not be brought to other parts of the buildings or to the grounds, and never to the student's own room or to the residence hall without the explicit permission of the Rector.

2 b. The special permission of the Rector is required to visit the room of a priest who is a guest of the Seminary. When this permission is given, it does not imply leave from class or any other common exercise.

Appendix B: Faculty

The faculty at St. Joseph's Seminary was made up almost entirely of priests of the Grand Rapids diocese. The rector was the priest in charge of running the seminary, a role similar to superintendent in today's public school system. The rector was appointed by the bishop of the Diocese of Grand Rapids, since the seminary was part of the bishop's jurisdiction. In the early days of the seminary the rector was also a professor but by the 1950's his responsibilities precluded any time for teaching.

Rectors

Rev. Anthony C. Volkert, July, 1909.
Rev. Charles D. White, November, 1919.
Rev. Thomas L. Noa, February, 1927.
Rev. Edmund F. Falicki, May, 1946.
Rev. James P. Moran, September, 1957.
Rev. Anthony C. Vainavicz, December, 1974.
Rev. Theodore J. Kozlowski, June 9, 1976.

Faculty

The names of the faculty are listed with their dates of assignment to the seminary where known. This information is taken from various issues of the *Recorder* and a list compiled in 1959 by Mitch Zellin, the Registrar, for the 50th anniversary of the seminary. I have listed them all as Rev. rather than the honorary titles they may have later received.

Rev. Gaspar Ancona, September 1963 -June 1966.
Rev. Anthony P. Arszulowicz, 1932-1941.
Rev. Raymond Baker, 1924-1938.
Mr. John E. Bellardo, 1944- June 1960.
Rev. Ernest J. Bernott, 1948-1949.
Rev. Edward J. Bielskas, 1944, 1950-1955.
Rev. Robert Bissot, 1962- June 1966.
Rev. Thomas Bolger, 1962- unknown date.
Rev. James A. Bryant, 1923-1936.
Rev. Joseph E. Ciesluk, 1944-1948.
Rev. George O. Dequoy, 1911-1916.
Rev. Raymond Drinan 1921-1922
    He left because of ill health. [314]
Rev. Edmund F. Falicki, 1930-June 1957.
Rev. Leo Farquharson, 1913-1924.
Rev. Noel P. Fay, January 1957- unknown date.
Rev. George Flanagan, 1911~1921.
Rev. Joseph Flickinger, 1965 – to unknown date.

Rev. Louis Flohe, 1926-1938.
He joined faculty to teach Latin and German and later was ordained. [315]
Mr. Merlin Fritzen, 1966 – to unknown date.
Rev. Michael J. Gallagher,1909-1911.
   Coadjutor Bishop of Grand Rapids, 1915-1916.
   Bishop of Grand Rapids 1916-1918.
   Bishop of Detroit 1918-1937.
Rev. Gerard F. Guzikowski, 1958 - to unknown date.
Rev. Francis L. Hackett, 1953-January 1957.
Mr. Frederick Hall, 1948-1949.
Rev. John P. Hoogterp, 1949-1954.
Rev. William J. Hoogterp, 1937-1948.
Rev. August Hovorka, 1920-1922.
He died in New Orleans while attending American Legion convention. [316]
Rev. Adam Joseph, 1951-1954.
Rev. Albert Kehren, 1921-1923.
Rev. Joseph E. Kohler, January 1927-1938.
Rev LaPres, Unknown start date - 1949.
Rev. David LeBlanc, 1964 – to unknown date.
Mr. Don Lennon, 1964 – to unknown date.
Rev. Thomas O. Martin, 1935-1938,1957- June 1966.
He became Michigan's first priest-civil-lawyer.[317]
Rev. John M. Matusas, 1948-1950.
Rev. John N. McDuffee, 1946-1948.
Rev. John McDuffee, 1966 – to unknown date.
Rev. John W. McGee, 1946-1948.
Rev. T. Vincent McKenna, 1938-1948.
Rev. Joseph C. McKinney, 1954- 1962.
   Auxiliary Bishop of Grand Rapids, 1968-2001.
Rev. William F. McKnight, 1948-1953.
Rev. James P. Moran 1945- December 1974.
Rev. S. J. Morrison, 1922-1929.
Rev. Joseph E. Murphy, 1943-1944.
Rev. William J.Murphy, 1933-1935.
Rev. Andrew Narloch, 1909-1912.
Rev. Stephen Narloch, 1912-1919.
Rev. Nieszwiecki, 1960 – to unknown date.
Rev. Clement Niedzwiecki, 1925-1932.
Rev. Thomas L. Noa, 1917-1946.
   Coadjutor Bishop of Sioux City, Iowa, 1946-1947.
   Bishop of Marquette 1947 - 1968.
Rev. George O'Brien, 1910-1912.

Mr. Karl Otto, unknown start date - to October 1926. [318]

Mr. Antos Pancurello, 2nd semester 1953.

Mr. G. Edward Philips, April - June 1953.

Rev. Emmeran L. Quaderer, 1936-1938.

Rev. Robert J. Rose, 1956 - to unknown date.
Bishop of Gaylord, 1981-1989, Grand Rapids, 1989-2003.

Rev. Leo S. Rosloniec, 1955- to unknown date.

Rev. John P. Ruba, 1915-1926.

Rev. Charles A. Salatka, 1944 – 1946.
Joined faculty when still a deacon. [319]
He was first alumnus of St. Joseph's to be named a bishop. [320]
Auxiliary Bishop of Grand Rapids, 1962-1968
Bishop of Marquette, 1968 - 1977.
Archbishop of Oklahoma City, 1977-1992.

Rev. Clement P. Sigmund, 1934-1938.

Rev. Henry Simon, 1922-1938.

Rev. Joseph E. Shaw, 1936- June 1966.

Rev. John F. Sonefeld, 1911-1919.

Rev. Speer Strahan, 1923-1924.

Rev. Raymond Sweeney, 1929-1932.

Rev. John J. Thome, 1946 - June 1965

Rev. Anthony Vainavicz, 1966 – to unknown date.

Rev. Louis VanBergen, 1949-1951.

Rev. Louis J. Verreau, 1933 - July 6, 1958.

Rev. Anthony Volkert, 1909-1943.
Rector Emeritus 1927-1943.

Rev . Donald Weiber, 1966 – to unknown date.

Rev. Joseph C. Walen, 1938-1943.

Rev John P. Weisengoff, 1957- to unknown date.

Rev. Charles D. White , 1911-1927.
Bishop of Spokane, Washington, 1927-1956.

Mr. E. E. Winters, 1939-1944.

Mr. Joseph Wisz, 1963 – to unknown date.

Rev. Joseph J. Zaskowski, 1946- to unknown date.

Rev. Herman H. Zerfas, 1948-1949.

Rev. William E. Zuidema, 1954 - June 1957.

Bibliography

Bulletin of St. Joseph's Seminary, 1956, 1962.

Honey, Charles and Dave Murray, "Diocese property sale falls through."*The Grand Rapids Press*, March 8, 2008.

"Look through the years – looking back.", *St. Joseph's Recorder*, March 1960.

Moore, Michael Langston, "Malinda Sapp dies from colon cancer; Statement released on the death of Marvin Sapp's wife", September 9, 2010. http://www.examiner.com/article/malinda-sapp-dies-from-colon-cancer-statement-released-on-the-death-of-marvin-sapp-s-wife

Murray, Dave, "Gospel star to open arts school ", *Grand Rapids Press*, March 11, 2008.

Prep Newsette, 1922-1928.

Rademacher, Tom. "St. Joseph's Seminary to Close Classrooms Still House Students" 1978

The Rule of St. Joseph's Seminary.
St. Joseph's Recorder, 1929-1932, 1938-1968.

Shellenbarger, Pat, "Pastor has big plans for Catholic property", *Grand Rapids Press*, October 21, 2007.

Williams, Tony, "St. Joseph's Seminary to Be Closed in June", *The Grand Rapids Press*, Grand Rapids, Michigan, March 4, 1981

Endnotes

1 St. Joseph's Recorder, May-June 1956.
2 *Bulletin* 1955.
3 *St. Joseph's Recorder,* Field Day insert 1954 or special issue.
4 ibid. May-June 1942.
5 ibid. May 1945.
6 ibid. June 1943.
7 ibid. June 1945.
8 ibid. June 1947.
9 ibid. June 1955.
10 ibid.,May-June 1956.
11 OpenHouse Newsletter 1957.
12 *St. Joseph's Recorder.*1965 Vol. 39, No. 4 (should be No. 5).
13 Field Day Newsletter, 1957.
14 Field Day Newsletter, 1957.
15 Scores for 1942-1955 were in the Field Day Newsletter for 1955.
16 St. Joseph's Recorder, May-June 1957.
17 ibid. May-June 1958.
18 ibid. May-June 1959.
19 ibid. May-June 1960.
20 ibid. May-June 1961.
21 ibid. Graduation 1962.
22 ibid. June 1963.
23 ibid. [1964] Vol. 38, No. 5.
24 ibid. May-June 1957.
25 ibid. May-June 1958.
26 ibid. May-June 1959.
27 ibid. May-June 1960.
28 ibid. May-June 1961.
29 ibid. Graduation 1962.
30 ibid. June 1963.
31 ibid. [1964] Vol. 38, No. 5.
32 ibid. [1965] Vol. 39, No. 4 (should be No. 5).
33 ibid. [1969] Vol. 43, No. 4.
34 ibid. September 1940.
35 ibid. February 1941.
36 ibid. September-October 1959.
37 *Prep Newsette,* April 7, 1922.
38 St. Joseph's Recorder, October 1939.
39 ibid. September-October 1959.
40 ibid. May 1946.
41 "Looking Back".

[42] *Prep Newsette*, October 20, 1923.

[43] *Bulletin*, 1925-26.

[44] *St. Joseph's Recorder*, November 1932.

[45] *The Rule*, Part II, Section III, Article 1.

[46] *The Rule*, Part II, Section III, Article 2 – Superiors.

[47] *Prep Newsette*, December 1925.

[48] *St. Joseph's Recorder*, October 1943.

[49] *St. Joseph's Recorder*, September-October 1958.

[50] ibid. Graduation 1962.

[51] ibid. [1965-1966] Vol. 41, No. 1.

[52] *Prep Newsette*, February 1922.

[53] *ibid.* October 1924.

[54] *ibid.* April 1925.

[55] *St. Joseph's Recorder*, November-December 1956.

[56] *Prep Newsette,* April 26, 1924.

[57] *ibid.* September 20, 1924.

[58] *Prep Newsette*, October 1928 and *St. Joseph's Recorder*, October 1929.

[59] *Bulletin* 1955.

[60] *St. Joseph's Recorder*, March 1954.

[61] ibid. [1964-1965] Vol. 39, No. 1.

[62] *Prep Newsette* October 1925.

[63] *St. Joseph's Recorder*, October 1943.

[64] ibid. November-December 1957.

[65] ibid. May-June 1958.

[66] *Prep Newsette,*May 1928.

[67] ibid. April 1928.

[68] *St. Joseph's Recorder*, May 1931.

[69] ibid.,September 1940.

[70] ibid.,November 1942.

[71] ibid. November 1943.

[72] ibid. February 1944.

[73] ibid. January 1940.

[74] ibid. January-February 1955 and January-February 1956.

[75] ibid.,April 1939.

[76] ibid. January 1940

[77] ibid. February 1940.

[78] ibid. February 1941.

[79] ibid. March 1942.

[80] ibid. April 1943.

[81] ibid. March 1944.

[82] ibid. June 1945.

[83] ibid. March-April1947.

[84] ibid. February 1948.

[85] ibid. January-February 1951.

[86] ibid. January-February 1952.

[87] ibid. Easter 1953.

[88] ibid. April 1954.

[89] ibid. March-April 1955.

[90] ibid. May-June 1957.

[91] ibid. March-April 1958.

[92] ibid. January-February 1959.

[93] ibid. March-April 1959.

[94] ibid. January-February 1960.

[95] ibid. "Debates head staff agenda", January –February 1961 and "Debates wind-up, Orations begin", March-April 1961

[96] ibid. Pre-Lenten 1962.

[97] ibid. January-February 1963.

[98] *Prep Newsette*, November 3, 1923

[99] *St. Joseph's Recorder*, May 1945.

[100] ibid. January-February 1951

[101] ibid. January-February 1952.

[102] ibid. September-October 1957.

[103] ibid. May-June 1958.

[104] ibid. March-April 1959.

[105] ibid. September-October 1959.

[106] ibid. September-October 1960.

[107] ibid. March-April 1961.

[108] ibid. Halloween 1961.

[109] ibid. Pre-Lenten 1962.

[110] ibid. March-April 1962.

[111] ibid. Halloween 1962.

[112] ibid. January-February 1963.

[113] ibid. March-April 1963.

[114] ibid. [1964-1965] Vol. 38, No. 1.

[115] ibid. [1964-1965] Vol. 38, No. 4.
[116] ibid. *St.Joseph's Recorder*, October 1939.
[117] *Prep Newsette*, December 1925.
[118] ibid. December 1926.
[119] ibid., November 1927.
[120] ibid. November 1928.
[121] *St. Joseph's* Recorder, December 1929.
[122] ibid. December 1930.
[123] ibid.,December 1931.
[124] ibid. December 1932.
[125] ibid. October 1939.
[126] ibid. November 1940.
[127] ibid. November 1942.
[128] ibid. November 1943.
[129] ibid. December 1944.
[130] ibid. January 1946.
[131] ibid. November 1947.
[132] ibid. December 1948.
[133] ibid. December 1949.
[134] ibid. Christmas 1951.
[135] ibid. Christmas 1952.
[136] ibid. December 1953.
[137] ibid. November-December 1954.
[138] ibid. November-December 1955.
[139] ibid. November-December 1956.
[140] ibid. November-December 1957..
[141] ibid. November-December 1959.
[142] ibid. November-December 1960.
[143] ibid. Christmas 1961.
[144] ibid. December 1962.
[145] ibid. [1964-65] Vol. 38, No. 2.
[146] ibid. [1965-66] Vol. 40, No. 2.
[147] *Prep Newsette*, January 1926.
[148] *St. Joseph's Recorder*, October 1930.
[149] ibid., October 1944.
[150] ibid., June 1955.
[151] ibid., Vol. 38, No. 1.

[152] ibid. February 1930.

[153] ibid., February 1944.

[154] ibid., December 1944.

[155] ibid. March-April 1947.

[156] ibid. March-April 1955.

[157] ibid. September-October 1957.

[158] *Prep Newsette*, February 26, 1922.

[159] *Prep Newsette*, February 24, 1923.

[160] *St. Joseph's Recorder*, November 1931.

[161] ibid., November 1938.

[162] ibid., January 1940.

[163] ibid., February 1944.

[164] ibid., May 1946.

[165] ibid. March-April 1959.

[166] ibid. March-April 1962.

[167] *Prep Newsette*, March 25, 1922.

[168] *Prep Newsette*, April 21, 1923

[169] *Prep Newsette*, May 11, 1922.

[170] ibid. May 1925

[171] *St. Joseph's Recorder*, June 1943.

[172] ibid. February 1945.

[173] ibid. September-October 1960.

[174] *Prep Newsette,* December 8, 1923.

[175] *Prep Newsette,* Christmas 1924.

[176] *St. Joseph's Recorder*, November 1940.

[177] ibid. March 1940.

[178] ibid., April 1945.

[179] ibid. Easter 1953.

[180] ibid. October 1953.

[181] ibid., April 1954.

[182] *Prep Newsette*, March 1928.

[183] *Prep Newsette*, April 22, 1922.

[184] *Prep Newsette*, April 22, 1922.

[185] *St. Joseph's Recorder*, February 1944.

[186] ibid. September-October 1958.

[187] ibid. September-October 1959.

[188] ibid. September-October 1960.

[189] ibid. Christmas 1961.

[190] ibid. 1963-1964 Vol. 38, No. 4..

[191] ibid. 1963-1964-Vol. 38, No. 1.

[192] ibid. 1964-65] Vol. 39, No. 2.

[193] ibid. 1965-1966 Vol. 40, No. 4.

[194] ibid. 1963-1964 Vol. 38, No. 3.

[195] ibid. 1964-65] Vol. 39, No. 1.

[196] ibid. 1964-65] Vol. 39, No. 2.

[197] ibid. 1965-1966 Vol. 40, No. 3.

[198] ibid. 1964 Vol. 38, No. 3.

[199] ibid. 1964-65] Vol. 39, No. 4 (should be No. 5).

[200] ibid. 1968-1969 Vol. 43, No. 4.

[201] ibid. 1963-1964 Vol. 38, No. 5.

[202] ibid. 1964-65] Vol. 39, No. 3.

[203] ibid. 1964-65] Vol. 39, No. 3, 1965-66 Vol. 40, No. 1, 1965-66 Vol. 40, No. 2, 1965-1966 Vol. 40, No. 3.

[204] ibid. [1964-65] Vol. 39, No. 4.

[205] ibid. 1964-65] Vol. 39, No. 4.

[206] ibid. 1964-65] Vol. 39, No. 4 (should be No. 5).

[207] ibid. 1965-1966 Vol. 40, No. 3.

[208] ibid. 1966-67 Vol. 41, No. 1.

[209] ibid. 1968-69 Vol. 43, No. 2.

[210] ibid. 1965-66 Vol. 40, No. 2.

[211] ibid. 1966-67 Vol. 41, No. 1.

[212] ibid. 1968-69 Vol. 43, No. 2.

[213] ibid. 1968-1969 Vol. 43, No. 3

[214] ibid. 1965-1966 Vol. 40, No. 4.

[215] ibid. 1968-1969 Vol. 43, No. 3.

[216] ibid. 1965-66 Vol. 40, No. 1.

[217] ibid. October 1943.

[218] ibid. October 1945.

[219] ibid. March-April 1963.

[220] *Prep Newsette*,June 15, 1922.

[221] ibid. September 16, 1922.

[222] ibid. September 22, 1923.

[223] ibid. September 20, 1924.

[224] ibid. October 1925.

[225] ibid. Commencement 1926.

[226] ibid. June 1927.

[227] *St. Joseph's Recorder*, June 1930.

[228] ibid. October 1930.

[229] ibid. October 1931.

[230] ibid. Commencement 1932.

[231] ibid. October 1938.

[232] ibid. May 1939.

[233] ibid. September 1939.

[234] ibid. May-June 1940.

[235] ibid. September 1940.

[236] ibid. May-June 1941.

[237] ibid. May-June 1942.

[238] ibid. October 1942.

[239] ibid. June 1943.

[240] ibid. October 1943.

[241] ibid. May-June 1944.

[242] ibid. October 1944.

[243] ibid. February 1945.

[244] ibid. October 1945.

[245] ibid. October 1945.

[246] ibid. October 1946.

[247] ibid. June 1947.

[248] ibid. June 1948.

[249] ibid. June 1949.

[250] ibid. October 1950.

[251] ibid. June 1951.

[252] ibid. June 1952.

[253] ibid. October 1952.

[254] *Bulletin* 1954-55, included 5 special students.

[255] ibid. September-October 1955 and letter from rector to finance board in December 1955.

[256] Included 6 HS and 6 college specials.

[257] ibid. September-October 1956.

[258] ibid. September-October 1957.

[259] *Bulletin* 1950-61 included 2 specials.

[260] "Look Through the Years"

[261] ibid.

[262] *St. Joseph's Recorder*, October 1942.

[263] *Prep Newsette*, May 11, 1922.

[264] *St. Joseph's Recorder*, November 1940.

[265] ibid. Easter 1952.

[266] *Bulletin* 1925-26.

[267] *St. Joseph's Recorder*, May-June 1961.

[268] ibid. November 1929.

[269] *Bulletin*, 1925-26.

[270] *St. Joseph's Recorder*, February 1944.

[271] *Prep Newsette*, December 1928.

[272] *St. Joseph's Recorder*, February 1947.

[273] *Prep Newsette*, April 1925 and October 1925

[274] *St. Joseph's Recorder*, December 1962.

[275] ibid. November 1945.

[276] ibid. Easter 1951 and May 1951.

[277] Personal note from Fr. Dennis Morrow.

[278] *Prep Newsette*, March 1928.

[279] *St. Joseph's Recorder*, November 1929.

[280] *Prep Newsette*, April 1925.

[281] *St. Joseph's Recorder*, March-April 1955.

[282] *Prep Newsette*, September 16, 1922.

[283] ibid. June 1926.

[284] *St. Joseph's Recorder*, March 1954.

[285] *St. Joseph's Recorder*, Halloween 1962.

[286] ibid. February 1942.

[287] ibid. October 1943.

[288] ibid. June 1946.

[289] ibid. October 1946 and Fr. John J. Thome.

[290] *St. Joseph's Recorder* 1964-76 Vol. 39, No. 1.

[291] *Prep Newsette*, November 1928.

[292] ibid. January-February 1955.

[293] *Prep Newsette*, December 1928, February 1929, April 1932.

[294] *St. Joseph's Recorder*, October 1930, September-October 1955.

[295] *St. Joseph's Recorder*, September-October 1955, September-October 1956.

[296] *St. Joseph's Recorder*, March-April 1956.

[297] *St. Joseph's Recorder*, May June 1957.

[298] Much of the information about the campus is taken from the *Bulletin* 1955-56 and 1962-63 unless otherwise noted.

[299] Personal note from Fr. Dennis Morrow.

[300] Inventory of assets, 1929 from the Archives of the Diocese of Grand Rapids.

[301] Tom Rademacher, "St. Joseph's Seminary to Close Classrooms Still House Students".

[302] Tony Williams, "St. Joseph's Seminary to Be Closed in June".

[303] "Look Back"

[304] Tony Williams, "St. Joseph's Seminary to Be Closed in June",

[305] ibid.

[306] ibid.

[307] Pat Shellenbarger, "Pastor has big plans for Catholic property".

[308] ibid.

[309] ibid.

[310] Dave Murray, "Grammy Nominee Plans To Start Academy At Former Catholic Diocese Site".

[311] ibid.

[312] Pat Shellenbarger, "Pastor has big plans for Catholic property."

[313] Michael Langston Moore, "Malinda Sapp dies from colon cancer."

[314] *St. Joseph's Recorder,* September 16, 1922.

[315] *Prep Newsette*, October 1926.

[316] *Prep Newsette*, November 11, 1922.

[317] *St. Joseph's Recorder*, January-February 1960.

[318] *Prep Newsette*, October 1926.

[319] *St. Joseph's Recorder*, February 1945.

[320] ibid. Pre-Lenten 1962.

Made in the USA
San Bernardino, CA
18 October 2015